Moving Forward Together

A Community Remembers 1898

Rhonda Bellamy
Editor

Si Cantwell
Assistant Editor

A Publication of the
1898 **Memorial Foundation**
Wilmington, North Carolina

Moving Forward Together

A Community Remembers **1898**

Rhonda Bellamy, Editor

Si Cantwell, Assistant Editor

A Publication of the

1898 **Memorial Foundation**

Contact and ordering information:

African-American Heritage Foundation of Wilmington
928 North 4th Street, Wilmington, NC 28401
telephone: (910) 262-8208

LIBRARY OF CONGRESS
CONTROL NUMBER: **2008935104**
Rhonda Bellamy, (editor) and Si Cantwell, (assistant editor)
Moving Forward Together - A Community Remembers 1898
Carolina Beach, N.C., SlapDash Publishing, LLC.
128 pp.

slapdash • publishing
LLC

311 Florida Avenue, Carolina Beach, NC 28428
910.232.0604 • slapdashpublishing@me.com
www.carolinabeach.net

First Printing: **November 2008**
Copyright © 2008 - 1898 Memorial Foundation

International Standard Book Number
978-0-9792431-5-8

This book and monument serve as a symbol of **Wilmington's commitment** to an inclusive society, a tribute to all who over the years have struggled **to reverse the tragic consequences** of the 1898 racial violence, and a memorial to those African-Americans killed in that violence.

1898 Foundation, Inc.

2008

Lethia Sherman Hankins, Co-chair

Laura W. Padgett, Co-chair

Robert Gerlach, Co-chair, 1898 Memorial Campaign

Bertha Boykin Todd, Co-chair, 1898 Memorial Campaign

Rosalind Moore Mosley, Secretary

Charlie West, Treasurer

Melton McLaurin, Assistant Treasurer

Earl Sheridan, Assistant Treasurer

Barbara Sullivan, Sculptor/Artist Liaison

Sherma Svitzer, Plaque Liaison

Hannah Vaughan, Plaque Liaison

Kenneth Davis, Resource

Becky Long, Exhibit

Mary Young, Campaign

Book Committee

Rhonda Bellamy

Si Cantwell

Paul Jefferson

Melton McLaurin

Bertha Boykin Todd

Public Relations Committee

Lethia Sherman Hankins

Paul Jefferson

Becky Long

Melton McLaurin

Earl Sheridan

Barbara Sullivan

Acknowledgments
Rhonda Bellamy, Editor

Life has a way of coming full circle. Little did I know in 1998 that I would edit a book in 2008 on the tragic events of 1898. Though I was co-executive secretary of the foundation during the centennial year, I was also a jaded journalist who'd seen too many well-intended efforts fall by the wayside – the casualties of time and limited resources. How heartened I am by the continued dedication of so many people who have worked to dispel the ominous shadow cast by the events of 1898. This book is an attempt to leave a living record of those great works.

The task was not mine alone. Star News columnist Si Cantwell wrote the 1898 history, assisted by LeRae Umfleet, principal researcher for the comprehensive 1898 Race Riot Commission Report, and Beverly Tetterton, local history librarian at the New Hanover County Public Library. The library also provided historic photos from the Hayden Collection. Si's section on Partners for Economic Inclusion was aided by Rob Gerlach, founding co-chairman, and 2008 chair Arlene Lawson.

Special thanks to:

Bertha Boykin Todd

1898 Executive Council

1898 Memorial Book Committee - Paul Jefferson, Melton McLaurin, Bertha Todd

John W. Davis III - Principal Photographer

Odeleye Studios

Wilmington Star News - Ken Blevins

Cape Fear Museum

New Hanover County Public Library

Gerald R. Parnell - University of North Carolina at Wilmington

Becky Long

Sherma Svitzer and Hannah Vaughan

Daniel Ray Norris, Publisher, SlapDash Publishing, LLC.

Bolton Anthony for his leadership and meticulous documentation

1898 Foundation Philosophy

"No one living in Wilmington today was a participant in the events of 1898. Consequently, none among us bears any personal responsibility for what happened.

But all among us – no matter our race or history, whether we have arrived here only recently or come from families that have called Wilmington home for generations – all among us are responsible for 1998. On each of us falls the personal responsibility to make our community one where economic justice and racial harmony flourish.

Surely this is a challenge we are willing to accept."

Bertha Boykin Todd

1898 Foundation Mission Statement

To "**tell the story**" of 1898 and make the real history known;

to "**heal the wounds**" of the racial division which continue in the city;

to "**honor the memory**" of those who lost lives and property in 1898; and

to "**restore the hope**" through efforts to foster economic inclusion.

Table of Contents

Foreword
Bertha Boykin Todd

Moving Forward Together

Those three words waved bravely from a banner at the opening ceremony of the centennial commemoration in 1998.

As I began speaking to people, both near and far, about our efforts to tell the story, heal the wound, honor the memory and restore the hope, the question would inevitably be asked, "Why is the foundation bringing up something that occurred one hundred years ago?"

"Those who cannot remember the past are condemned to repeat it," wrote George Santayana in *The Life of Reason* in 1906.

Faced with the options of remembering or repeating, the community chose to remember. The foundation set to the task in 1996 under the co-chairmanship of Dr. Bolton Anthony and Attorney William "Bill" Fewell. When Bill relocated to Pittsburgh, PA, I reluctantly agreed to serve as co-chair. I knew then that tremendous work lie ahead, chiefly, opening hearts and minds.

Fortunately, many Wilmingtonians did open their hearts and minds. They offered their talents and shared their financial resources. More than a decade later, we have a new hope, a new park, and a new story to tell.

The book *Moving Forward Together* is a record of a revisited history and a testament to the thoughts and feelings of many as we continue to journey through the 21st century together.

Moving Forward Together. Those three words still wave to those of us who - more than a decade later - carry forth the mantle of truth and reconciliation.

Bertha Boykin Todd
Former Co-chair, 1898 Centennial Foundation
Co-chair, 1898 Memorial Campaign

Introduction
Racial Violence in Wilmington, 1898
Melton McLaurin, Professor Emeritus, UNC Wilmington

While Wilmington's racial violence of 1898 is not unique, it represents an egregious example of the means by which the white South disenfranchised and imposed a strict form of racial segregation upon its African-American population at the turn of the twentieth century. The region established this system of Jim Crow primarily through the use of violence, the threat of violence, fraud, and economic coercion. Employing the same methods, the white South maintained this system until well into the seventh decade of the twentieth century.

The reasons for Wilmington's racial violence mirror those that fueled white supremacy campaigns throughout the South. Engrossed in the building of a modern industrial economy, the North had long abandoned its passion to protect the interest of the African-American population it had freed with the Civil War. White supremacy beliefs shared by white Northerners and Southerners helped justify America's plunge into imperialism with the 1898 Spanish American War, concluded only months before the Wilmington events. And throughout the South, and especially in North Carolina, a radical coalition of Republicans and members of the Populist Party, employing an appeal for political and economic unity between working class whites and blacks, challenged the power of the Democratic Party.

North Carolina's large and aggressive Populist Party fused with the Republicans to capture control of the state legislature in 1894. This Fusionist majority rewrote the state's election laws, significantly increasing black participation in state and local politics for the first time since Reconstruction. As a result, the Republicans elected Daniel Russell of Wilmington governor in 1896, and the Fusionists retained control of the state legislature while winning control of a number of municipal governments, including that of Wilmington.

This challenge to Conservative Democratic control of North Carolina politics led to a furious, highly emotional Democratic counterattack in 1898, one based largely on an appeal to white voters' fear of "Negro domination." Orchestrated by Furnifold M. Simmons of New Bern, State Democratic Party chairman, and Josephus Daniels, editor of the *Raleigh News and Observer*, the state's most influential Democratic newspaper, the campaign employed Wilmington as a symbol of "Negro domination." Wilmington was a logical choice, since by 1898 the city had an African-American majority with a large and rapidly expanding black middle class, and blacks served in both the municipal government and civil service.

The efforts of one member of Wilmington's black middle class to refute Democratic charges fueled the 1898 white supremacy campaign. Alexander Manly, editor of Wilmington's *Daily Record*, the state's only black daily, challenged the Democratic charge that black rapists threatened "white civilization." Manly asserted that many black men fell victim when white women discovered in consensual relationships with them cried rape. He challenged white men to be more protective of white women against sexual advances from males of all races. In preparation for the November 8 elections, Wilmington's Democratic press carried Manly's editorial daily in a successful effort to inflame white voter fears.

In the racially charged municipal election on November 8, 1898, the Democrats, by employing a campaign of open intimidation against black voters, won overwhelmingly. While Democratic leaders had avoided election day violence for fear of federal intervention, after the election others determined to immediately oust the biracial city council. On November 10 an armed mob of whites led by some of Wilmington's most respected and influential citizens destroyed Alexander Manly's *Daily Record* by burning the building in which it was housed. They then turned their fury and guns on the city's black population, killing at least ten blacks according to the contemporary white press, scores according to the oral tradition within the African-American community. The mob then drove others, perhaps hundreds – men, women and children – from their homes into surrounding lowlands in search of safety.

Over the next two days, as Wilmington's black citizens unsuccessfully appealed to the federal government for protection, groups of armed whites expelled from the city black and white political and business leaders opposed to Conservative Democratic rule and white supremacy. Armed whites under the leadership of the city's white elite used the threat of paramilitary forces to remove from office Wilmington's duly elected, biracial city government, replacing it with representatives of the old elite in what has been called the only successful coup d'etat in the United States. The failure of the federal government to protect the rights and lives of Wilmington's African-American citizens sent an unmistakable signal to the entire South that whites could employ violence against blacks with impunity. Using Wilmington as an example, in 1900 the Democratic Party carried out a state wide white supremacy campaign which returned the Conservative Democrats to power and resulted in the adoption of a new state constitution which disenfranchised African-Americans and countenanced the creation of a legally segregated society.

Courtesy New Hanover Public Library

3rd St Cross mark when 2 Negros were killed

L to R: **Sherma Svitzer, Earl Sheridan, Mayor Pro Tem Jim Quinn, Lethia S. Hankins, NCDOT Division Engineer Allen Pope, Laura W. Padgett, Bertha Todd, Barbara Sullivan, Kenneth Davis.**

photo by John W. Davis

Letter to the Community

The Vision Behind the Creation of the 1898 Memorial Park

The 1898 Memorial Park offers a rare opportunity to grasp again a vision once shared over a century ago by the citizens of Wilmington, North Carolina. The vision was of a city which, although knowing its share of economic hardship, offered a future of prosperity and progress to all who claimed the vision as their own and the city as their home.

As history has told us, the original vision for a growing, progressive Wilmington was dashed in the racial violence of November 1898. Diversity of race and class became a catalyst which ignited and, in one day, destroyed the tenuous race relations which then existed in the growing Port City. The incident fragmented race relations in Wilmington for decades to come.

The purpose behind the creation of the 1898 Memorial Park is to restore the promise of racial progress and to salute forward-looking residents of Wilmington. In this way the city once again stands as a mecca for many races, colors and creeds who seek a new life in the South - a South aware of its past but more focused on the future - a South not of what was but of what will be.

The design of the proposed memorial by Ayokunle Odeleye is very different than the existing historical landmarks and monuments in the city. Its commemorative symbolism offers full accessibility to the public. Rather than a rigid statue, this public art space opens a new gateway to the city and makes the 1898 Memorial Park a landmark of reconciliation. It will redefine Wilmington's history and new sense of self as a community in this new century.

As public art the new memorial will embody the sense of collective memory, shared history and vibrant future available to all who pass through its open-air space. Growing out of our community desire to remember, value, and learn from the troubles of the past, the memorial can be a visible and tangible symbol that unites rather than divides, heals rather than wounds, accepts rather than rejects. It can be a dramatic yet simple symbol of tolerance and understanding which once was lost but now has been found for Wilmington's future.

In Wilmington where history pulls and preys upon the present, the events of 1898 have for too long been a thorn in the civic pride of this historic city. Gracefully and without rancor the 1898 Memorial Park will permanently salute the sacrifices and contributions of the black and white citizens of southeastern North Carolina and reflect the progressive character, diversity and vibrancy of the region.

1898 MEMORIAL PARK – WILMINGTON, N.C.
PLAN VIEW @ THIRD STREET

Symbolism of the Paddle Sculptures

The six bronze sculptures represent paddles. They refer symbolically to water, an important element in the spiritual belief system of people from the African continent who resided in Wilmington during the 1800s. In many African traditions water was believed to be a medium for the transition from the world of the living to the realm of the dead and vice-versa. Crossing over a body of water in a boat using a paddle was believed to be a part of the deceased's journey into the next life. Anthropologists have documented that many Africa Americans from colonial times maintained these ancient beliefs. Evidence of this is seen in graveyard decorations from the period which are replete with water symbolism. The use of paddle imagery in this memorial pays homage to the African Americans who lost their lives in the 1898 violence.

Ayokunle Odeleye

1898 Memorial Park Inscription

In 1898 Wilmington's African-American majority included members of a growing middle class who served in the municipal government, the city's civil service, and in state and federal governmental positions. On November 10, 1898, an armed mob of whites led by some of Wilmington's most prominent citizens removed from office the city's duly elected biracial government in what historians consider the only successful coup d'etat in the history of the United States.

Between 1894 and 1896, a Republican-Populist coalition took control of the state government and several city governments, in part by appealing to African-Americans. Democrats initiated a counterattack in 1898, appealing to white voters' racial fears and portraying Wilmington, then the state's largest city, as an example of the dangers of "Negro rule." The Democratic press depicted African-American males as a threat to "Southern womanhood," a charge denied by Alexander Manly's *Record*, the state's only daily black newspaper.

The day following the elections of November 8, a white mob gathered at the courthouse and adopted the "White Man's Declaration of Independence." It demanded that the city return to an all white administration, that the *Record* cease publication and that Alex Manly be banished. White leaders presented the "Declaration" to prominent African-Americans, demanding a response within twelve hours. Mailed rather than hand delivered, their reply arrived too late.

On the morning of November 10, a mob of armed whites burned the *Record* to the ground, then turned its fury and guns on the city's African-American population. At least ten blacks died in the violence, scores more according to African-American oral tradition. Hundreds of men, women, and children fled to surrounding swamps and forests in search of safety. Whites expelled from the city both black and white political and business leaders who were opposed to Democratic rule and white supremacy. The federal government ignored African-American appeals for protection, signaling Democrats throughout the South that it would no longer protect blacks from white violence.

Wilmington's 1898 racial violence was not accidental. It began a successful statewide Democratic campaign to regain control of state government, disenfranchise African-Americans, and create a system of legal segregation which persisted into the second half of the 20th century.

This monument serves as a symbol of Wilmington's commitment to an inclusive society, a tribute to all who over the years have struggled to reverse the tragic consequences of the 1898 racial violence, and a memorial to those African-Americans killed in that violence.

photo by Daniel Ray Norris

The Making of a Monument
by Rhonda Bellamy

Sculptor Ayokunle Odeleye is never more than a stone's throw away from his life's work. Adjacent to his suburban Atlanta home sits a 30 x 40 foot metal fabrication studio where he gives "physical form to ideas." A separate 100 x 25 foot wood studio is located nearby.

After pulling another all-nighter and grabbing a power nap, he describes the process – likening construction of a maquette to "building a house with tweezers" and the finished product to "birthing a baby."

The babies – six imposing 16-foot skeletal structures made of carbon steel tubing and stainless steel braces – wait to be encased in cast bronze skin. They will become the paddles that anchor Wilmington's 1898 Memorial Park.

Transforming the barren triangular tract of land into a space of beauty and a site for reconciliation required thought. He trekked the 375 miles from Atlanta to Wilmington on fact-finding missions. Armed with a sketch pad and a notebook, he talked with area residents about the historic event that prompted an international solicitation for a fitting monument.

photo by John W. Davis

"I go into the environment and take note of all its components," said the Kennesaw State art professor, who added that there is a difference between public art and art being put in public places.

The legwork paid off. The 1898 Memorial Committee, co-chaired by Laura W. Padgett and Harvard Jennings, received 66 applications. Three finalists were selected by a panel of local art historians and artists, including the late Ren Brown, director of Cameron Art Museum, Don Fishero, director of the defunct Arts Council of the Lower Cape Fear, playwright Anne Russell, and musician/ storyteller Lloyd Wilson. Models from the three finalists were displayed, and the artists made presentations at Cape Fear Museum in November 2000.

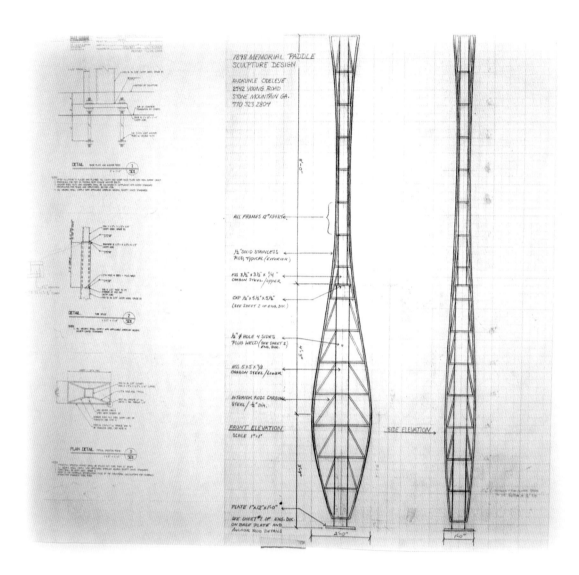

The Odeleye Group maquette, designed by Odeleye, Marianne Weinberg-Benson, and the landscape architects at jon Benson + associates, inc., was the overwhelming favorite among the seven-member 1898 panel who voted on it, and among the general public ballots collected at the New Hanover County Public Library where the models were displayed.

"The paddles refer symbolically to water, an important element in the spiritual belief system of people from the African continent and their descendants who resided in Wilmington during the 1800s," wrote Odeleye.

"The simplicity of the design is very powerful. He understood we didn't want to point fingers but we wanted to acknowledge what happened and move forward," said 1898 spokesperson Bertha Todd.

22

Courtesy of Odeleye Studios

Courtesy of Odeleye Studios

Odeleye and his team arrived in Wilmington on July 11, 2008 to install the sculptural elements of the 1898 Memorial Park. Each of the six paddles weighs about 1000 pounds.

Arched stonework forms the platform for the memorial's historical inscription and recognition of major donors.

As the new gateway into downtown Wilmington via I-40, the site at Third and Davis streets is located one block from where the initial casualties of 1898 took place.

The park's official dedication will be held on November 8, 2008, 110 years after the racial violence of 1898.

Odeleye's larger-than-life renderings "help communities find identity." In 2007 he installed two 16-foot-tall, freestanding stainless steel statues in Spring Valley, New York, a community where 37 languages are spoken by its 22,000 citizens. Flanking the entrance to Memorial Park, the "Spring Valley Twins" have the same inscription carved into their bases in different languages, "Our differences make us a unique and culturally rich community."

Trained at Virginia Commonwealth University in Richmond, Virginia, and at Howard University in Washington, D.C., Odeleye received a BFA degree from Howard University in 1973 and the MFA degree in 1975.

Though his love of art began with drawing and painting, Odeleye soon developed a passion for three-dimensional art under the tutelage of Howard University sculpture professor Ed Love.

Love often told Odeleye to envision the end result or "the final solution." But the road from idea to final solution is as much mechanical as it is artistic. Odeleye has taught himself arc and mig welding as well as the woodworking skills needed "to produce physical manifestations of things conceived in the mind's eye and released into the realm of tangible form."

He has been teaching art since 1973, holding positions at Dunbar High School, The Duke Ellington School for the Arts, Howard University, Spelman College, Woodland Middle School, Georgia State University and Kennesaw State University.

Odeleye is a tenured professor of art at Kennesaw University, where he has taught since 1989. In addition to three-dimensional design, he teaches African-American art history, art appreciation, drawing, and sculpture.

Other Public Art Commissions and Grants
Partial Listing for Sculptor Ayokunle Odeleye

2005-2007 COMMISSION, Rockland County Art In Public Places Program, New York. Two 16ft.h stainless steel free standing sculptures for the city of Spring Valley New York.

2004 COMMISSION Alaska State Council on the Arts. A 14ft.h x 14ft.w wood and mixed media wall relief sculpture for the Alaska Psychiatric Institute in Anchorage Alaska

2002 COMMISSION, Prince Georges County Art in Public Places Program. A monumental stainless steel free standing sculpture with seating for the Bunker Hill fire station in Mt. Rainer Maryland.

2002 COMMISSION, Hartsfield Atlanta International Airport. Atlanta, Georgia. A wood relief sculpture for the Immigrations corridor on Concourse E.

2001 COMMISSION, 1898 Memorial Foundation, Wilmington, North Carolina. A monumental environmental sculpture memorial park to commemorate the coup d'etat of 1898. The sculpture memorial designed for Wilmington includes bronze and stone elements as well as sculptural landscaping.

2001 COMMISSION, St. Petersburg Bureau of Cultural Affairs, St. Petersburg, Florida. A 10ft.h x 12ft.w stainless steel sculpture for the Wildwood Recreation Center.

2000 COMMISSION, Fulton County Arts Council, Atlanta, Georgia. Two 5ft.h x 12ft.l stainless steel wall relief sculptures for the Adams Park Library in Atlanta, Georgia.

1999 GRANT AWARD, Fulton County Arts Council, Atlanta, Georgia. Worked with Magnet Arts High School students at North Springs High School in creating a large wood relief sculpture.

1997 COMMISSION, Clayton College and State University, Morrow, Georgia. A 14ft stainless steel sculpture with stainless seating for the college's campus.

1996/97 COMMISSION, City of Richmond Public Art Commission, Richmond, Virginia. Three 6 x 6 carved panels for the courthouse lobby.

1995/96 COMMISSION, Atlanta Committee for the Olympic Games. A monumental bronze sculpture for an Olympic stadium community in Atlanta, Georgia in conjunction with the 1996 Olympic Games.

1996 COMMISSION, Baltimore City College High School, Baltimore, Maryland. A 20ft.h x 12ft.w x 6ft.d steel sculpture which involved collaboration with engineers, contractors and architects.

1995 COMMISSION, Morehouse College, Atlanta Georgia. A ceremonial throne to be occupied by the new President of Morehouse College during the colleges 1996 inauguration ceremonies.

1995 COMMISSION, City of Atlanta Bureau of Cultural Affairs, Atlanta, Georgia. A 14ft. stainless steel sculpture for a park in the Martin Luther King historic district.

1995 COMMISSION, Dallas Area Rapid Transit Authority, Dallas, Texas. A 14ft.h x 18ft. l bronze sculpture for a newly built rail station.

1992 COMMISSION, Martin Luther King Memorial Commission of Pensacola Florida. A bronze bust of Dr. King for an outdoor plaza park area in Pensacola, Florida.

1990 COMMISSION, Georgia Council for the Arts. A wood relief sculpture for Spelman College.

photo by John W. Davis

1898 Foundation Co-Chairs, Lethia S. Hankins and Laura W. Padgett,
prepare for a press conference prior to installation of the park's
sculptural elements in July 2008.

State and City Support New Gateway

By the end of the centennial year, co-chairs Laura W. Padgett and Bertha Todd began meeting with the North Carolina Department of Transportation (NCDOT) about the proposed site for the 1898 Memorial Park. They secured an agreement to acquire the triangular plot at North Third and Davis streets, where the Martin Luther King Parkway (then Smith Creek Parkway) would enter the city on the north side. The State, which would construct and landscape the proposed park, would own the land until it was deeded to the City of Wilmington. The City of Wilmington agreed to maintain the site and monument in perpetuity.

In 1999 Wilmington City Council authorized the foundation to act as its liaison with NCDOT. Jeff Lackey of the Landscape Design and Development Division of the NCDOT and Allen Pope, Division Engineer for NCDOT, served as principal liaisons, offering design and technical support, but leaving all major design decisions to the foundation. The project had become a cooperative effort among the local community, NCDOT, and the Department of Cultural Resources, which provided a $10,000 grant to plan the project.

Fundraising Campaign Hits Goal

At the conclusion of the centennial year, the 1898 Foundation's Executive Council decided to concentrate on the chief remaining goal – to "honor the memory" with an 1898 Memorial Park. The foundation established an 1898 Memorial Fund with the Cape Fear Community Foundation and began the public campaign to raise a projected $200,000. Members of the committee included Rob Gerlach, Lethia Hankins, Paul Jefferson, Herb McKim, Melton McLaurin, Jim and Marjorie Megivern, Yvonne Pagan, Thomas Schmid, Earl Sheridan, Barbara Sullivan, Sherma Svitzer, Bertha Todd, and Charles West. The silent phase of the campaign was mounted during the summer of 2000. The campaign went public on September 27, 2000 at a press conference at Cape Fear Museum. Through December 10, 2000, the first phase of the campaign resulted in pledges totaling $163,000, including Founders Circle pledges ($10000) and several Peace Circle pledges ($5000). The goal was reached in mid-2008.

Wilmington Mayors and the 1898 Memorial

by Paul R. Jefferson

Since 1997 Wilmington mayors have supported 1898 commemorative efforts and the 1898 Memorial Park. Their individual efforts were in marked contrast with those of mayors Silas P. Wright and Alfred Waddell, who presided during the city's political and racial conflict 110 years ago.

During the term of Mayor Don Betz, in office from 1987-1997, initial legislation was passed to create the citywide group known as the 1898 Reconciliation Committee in 1997. "It took some time to get it in front of the City Council, but I felt it was important. 1898 was a difficult time in city history, and it should be remembered," Betz said.

In 1998 Mayor Hamilton Hicks worked with 1898 Executive Committee member Kenneth Davis to "set the tone" for the well-attended biracial gatherings and discussions held throughout the city during the centennial year. "We wanted to focus on the common threads of understanding the riot, not to create animosity or more anxiety. We needed to recognize that it occurred both from a historical viewpoint and for what it means for Wilmingtonians today. We wanted to make certain that the idea (of a memorial) stayed alive," said Hicks.

Mayor David Jones continued the pattern of support established by his predecessors. "It's important to re-establish what a good community we have. The black community was an important part of Wilmington then, as it is now. The memorial is a good tribute to the city."

During his term, Mayor Harper Peterson likewise saluted the 1898 effort. Peterson served on the 1898 Race Riot Commission, a state-level committee appointed by the General Assembly to officially document the long-hidden chapter of the racial violence, labeled by historians as the only successful coup d'etat of a duly elected government in the United States. "It's a fine memorial, and we need to do more to restore the economic and commercial concerns that remain in the black community," Peterson said.

Mayor Spence Broadhurst thought the site at N. Third and Davis streets was a prime location given the resurgence of Wilmington's northern downtown area. The city had already pledged its resources to maintain the memorial park land in perpetuity.

Citing the importance of the 1898 Memorial, current Mayor Bill Saffo sees the realization of the long-planned memorial as a visible sign of reconciliation among Wilmingtonians. He pledged to continue the role of the Office of the Mayor of Wilmington in setting the tone for outreach, civility and camaraderie among Wilmington residents of every color.

photos by John W. Davis

photos by John W. Davis

A History of the 1898 Racial Violence

Si Cantwell, Assistant Editor

Some effects of the events of November 10, 1898, when murderous white mobs rampaged through the city killing black people and driving them from their homes, businesses and political offices, still linger in the city.

In 1897, Wilmington had a racially diverse economy and political structure, supported by a vibrant African-American community living and working alongside whites. The hatred, fear and violence that developed as a result of the 1898 political campaign created a new Wilmington, one in which older black people whispered recollections of 1898 to younger generations, creating a lasting fear.

Resentments have endured, feeding into a sense of distrust that contributed to Wilmington's other epochal racial clash, when a school boycott by black students during desegregation led to a night of fires and gunshots in February 1971. Ten people – nine black men and one white woman – were convicted and imprisoned. Their convictions were overturned by the U.S. Fourth Circuit Court of Appeals on Dec. 4, 1980.

In 1998, black and white people in Wilmington came together to commemorate the events of 1898 and try to heal its lingering wounds. The General Assembly of North Carolina passed a bill creating the 1898 Wilmington Race Riot Commission, which produced The 1898 Wilmington Race Riot Report, an official history of the event. LeRae Umfleet of the Research Branch of the state Office of Archives and History wrote the account.

This is a condensed version of that history.

Umfleet starts by describing Wilmington just before the Civil War.

In 1860, wealthy plantation owners occupied the top rung of the local hierarchy. Next down were merchants and businessmen. Then came the white working class, skilled artisans and unskilled laborers. Free blacks and slaves composed the bottom of the social scale.

Before the Civil War, Wilmington had a large free black population. Many blacks had skilled positions such as carpenters and masons. But the largest group of black Wilmington residents was African-American slaves. Some worked for the railroad or in maritime trades, some were domestic servants of wealthy Wilmingtonians. Others were skilled artisans, some of whom made money for their masters and even themselves by hiring out their talents.

After the Civil War and Emancipation, many of these skilled black workers became prosperous. Wilmington's population grew as residents came from the surrounding countryside and from the north looking for jobs.

The city's economy rebounded quickly from the ravages of the war and its aftermath, when Wilmington was occupied by Federal troops.

In the Reconstruction era, which lasted from the end of the Civil War until 1877, the United States Constitution was amended to abolish slavery, to grant citizenship to blacks and to give black men the right to vote.

In Wilmington, the U.S. military occupied the city after the war and took control of its government. The Federal government also established the Freedmen's Bureau to ease the transition from slavery to citizenship. Many among Wilmington's large black population became active in Republican politics.

On the state level, the decades between the Civil War and the events of 1898 saw power struggles between a conservative Democratic party representing the interests of the former white ruling class and a more liberal Republican party, supported by blacks and whites.

Black people prospered in Wilmington and by the 1880s were holding Emancipation Day ceremonies with parades and speeches by blacks and whites alike.

There were black literary societies and libraries. By the 1890s, black people played prominent roles in Wilmington's economic and political circles.

A new Populist Party joined with Republicans in a coalition called Fusion, which in 1894 won a majority in the General Assembly. Locally, crafty Republicans led by Brunswick County native Daniel Russell won all the races in which the party fielded candidates.

Election laws were changed to favor Fusion politicians and black voters, to the detriment of Democratic politicians. Russell became governor in the 1896 election. Wilmington's city elections of March 1897 went smoothly, with two black Republicans and three white Democrats elected. Local blacks continued to make gains in business and education.

But the run-up to the election of November 8, 1898, became ugly as white Democrats resolved to regain power.

Furnifold Simmons, chairman of the state Democratic campaign, plotted a strategy using men who could "write, speak and ride."

The writers wrote white supremacy propaganda for many of the state's newspapers including Wilmington's *Morning Star* and the *Messenger*, the *Raleigh News and Observer* and the *Charlotte Observer*. Incendiary editorial cartoons reinforced the white supremacy rhetoric, depicting the Negro as a vampire crushing powerless white people or as a devil whispering in a voter's ear.

Speakers such as Charles B. Aycock spread similar messages throughout the state, inflaming white voters by playing on their fears and post-Civil War resentments. Wilmington native Alfred Moore Waddell alleged that Fusion rule was unjust. In an influential speech on October 24 at Thalian Hall, Waddell said of black people, "the mass of them are ignorant and ... have been played upon and preyed upon by vicious leaders of their own race and by mean white men."

"Let them understand once and for all that we will have no more of the intolerable conditions under which we live. We are resolved to change them, if we have to choke the current of the Cape Fear with carcasses," he proclaimed. "Negro domination shall henceforth be only a shameful memory to us and an everlasting warning to those who shall ever again seek to revive it. To this declaration we are irrevocably committed and true men everywhere will hail it with a hearty Amen!"

The men who could ride joined groups such as the Red Shirts, a movement that had originated in South Carolina. Brightly garbed bands of men rode through neighborhoods waving pistols and rifles, spreading fear. They became "effectively a terrorist arm of the Democratic Party," Umfleet wrote.

As the state's largest city, Wilmington was a focal point for this three-pronged strategy. The Republican and Populist Fusion coalition could do little against the well-organized effort, especially after their leaders were threatened with personal violence.

Gov. Russell traveled from Raleigh to Wilmington to vote on Election Day 1898. As he was returning, his train was stopped and boarded by Red Shirts in Hamlet and Maxton. Fearing for his safety, railroad officials hid the governor in a baggage car.

A group of Democrats called the "Secret Nine" had been organized in Wilmington, ostensibly planning protection for white women and children, but also planning the coup d'etat of November 10.

Another group of white businessmen formed the Group of Six. Eventually the two groups merged with the official Democratic Party, the Democrats' White Government Union and the Red Shirts. The city's Chamber of Commerce, the Merchant's Association and the Wilmington Light Infantry also became allied with the white supremacy movement.

The speeches and newspaper articles led Wilmington's white citizens to fear a violent uprising by black people. Some whites sent their wives and children out of the city.

The writers, speakers and Red Shirt riders inspired "a state of terror" among the black citizenry, according to one observer.

As Election Day approached, violence began to seem inevitable. Col. Roger Moore began drilling paramilitary units of white men.

Amid all this tension, Alexander Manly, editor of the Wilmington *Record*, wrote an editorial in August 1898 that would result in the destruction of his newspaper. *The Record* was the city's only African-American newspaper. Manly, a mulatto who was a descendant of Gov. Charles Manly, used his newspaper to push for improvements for the black community in Wilmington.

Alex Manly

His editorial came in response to an 1897 speech by a Rebecca L. Felton of Georgia urging that black males accused of raping white women be lynched.

Umfleet says Manly wrote the editorial after Felton's speech was reprinted in Wilmington newspapers.

Manly countered that white women "are not any more particular in the matter of clandestine meetings with colored men than are the white men with colored women," and that it was "no worse for a black man to be intimate with a white woman, than for a white man to be intimate with a colored woman."

"Every Negro lynched," Manly wrote, "is called a 'big, burly, black brute' when in fact many of those who have thus been dealt with had white men for their fathers and were not only not 'black' and 'burly' but were sufficiently attractive for white girls of culture and refinement to fall in love with them as is very well known to all."

VILE AND VILLAINOUS

Outrageous Attack on White Women by a Negro Paper Published in Wilmington.

Weeks later, Democratic officials started quoting Manly's editorial. Other newspapers called it a horrid slander against white women and began writing about it every day. Rumors circulated that Manly would be lynched if he didn't leave town.

November 8 brought Election Day, with a record turnout statewide. In Wilmington, there were no gunshots, but bands of armed men intimidated black and Republican voters. Members of the White Government Union were posted at polling places with instructions to ignore voter fraud.

The vote count was also marked by ballot stuffing. After a scuffle that extinguished the lights at one Republican-majority precinct, it was found that nearly 200 more votes were cast than there were people registered in the district. The Democrats won overwhelmingly.

That night, the Wilmington Light Infantry stood ready to repel an assault by black people. No such assault came.

The next day, November 9, whites held a series of meetings calling for the mayor and chief of police to resign. The resulting White Declaration of Independence demanded white rule of the city, more jobs for white workers, that the *Record* cease publication and that Manly leave town. A Committee of Twenty-Five, chaired by orator Alfred Moore Waddell, presented these demands to the Committee of Colored Citizens, a group of men deemed leaders of the black community – civic, religious, and business leaders.

The black representatives came to a meeting at 6 p.m. on November 9 and were given until 7:30 a.m. the next morning to say if they would comply "without the use of strong measures."

Col. Moore's men patrolled overnight as the city awaited the answer from the Committee of Colored Citizens.

The answer never came.

Reply of the Colored Committee to "The White Declaration of Independence"
The Committee of Colored Citizens to Hon. A.M. Waddell, undated typewritten copy in Alfred M. Waddell Papers, Southern Historical Collection, University of North Carolina Library.

Dear Sir,
We the colored citizens to whom was referred the matter of expulsion from this community, of the persons and press of A.M. Manly, beg most respectfully to say that we are in no wise responsible for nor in any way endorse the obnoxious article that called forth your activities. Neither are we authorized to act for him in this matter, but in the interest of peace we will most willingly use our influence to have your wishes carried out.
Very respectfully,
The Committee of Colored Citizens

Wilmington Light Infantry Armory

Newspapers reported the fateful morning of November 10 that Manly had left the city and that the *Record* had suspended publication.

Some white leaders received assurances from black committee members that Manly was leaving and that a response would be presented to Waddell.

But those white leaders weren't present when Waddell arrived at the Wilmington Light Infantry (WLI) armory on Market Street around 8:15 a.m.

Waddell was met by a crowd of 500, many of them excited and exhausted from overnight patrols and the weeks of rising tension. He told them there had been no reply from the black committee.

The crowd became restive, with calls to march on the *Record's* office.

So Waddell led them in military-style columns, four wide and two city blocks deep, toward the press. Residents watched from their porches. As the crowd turned off Market Street onto Seventh Street and crossed Orange Street,

the neighborhood became mostly black. Those residents stayed inside, watching the hour-long procession of 1,000 to 1,500 men.

The *Record's* press was in a building called Love and Charity Hall near Seventh and Nun streets. Waddell knocked on the door but received no answer. The men broke in and began destroying the press and other equipment. A fire started, most likely when hanging kerosene laps were knocked to the floor.

The violence of 1898 was under way.

Fire crews were prevented from working at the building until it was damaged beyond repair.

Black children ran through the streets in panic as an older woman "invoked the wrath of Heaven" on the perpetrators.

Waddell and the men returned to the WLI armory, and he told them to go quietly home. But it was too late. Bands of armed white men were already roving the city.

The Brooklyn neighborhood saw the worst of the day's violence.

Black workers at Sprunt Cotton Compress, on the river between Walnut and Red Cross streets, heard about the burning of the *Record* and gathered outside the compress.

Owner James Sprunt tried to get them to go home, but large numbers of armed whites arrived. Tension ensued amid calls to "kill the whole band of negroes." Sprunt protected his workers and eventually many were escorted home by groups of armed white men.

Other black waterfront workers tried to get to their homes but were turned back by armed white patrols.

Some of the men who had burned the *Record* boarded a streetcar and rode it south on Sixth Street and west along Castle Street to Front Street, where it turned north. They fired rifle shots into black homes and businesses.

Black waterfront workers confronted armed whites at Fourth and Harnett in Brooklyn.

As some blacks and whites tried to calm the citizens and get them to go home, armed whites began showing up.

Accounts differ on who fired the first shot, but soon whites were firing at a crowd of blacks in front of W.A. Walker's store at Fourth and Harnett. Several black men were wounded and it appears at least three were killed instantly. Two others ran into a house a 411 Harnett, where one died.

A running firefight ensued on Harnett Street. Whites began firing in unison at a group of black men, killing five or six more of them near Fourth and Harnett.

A white man was wounded by a stray bullet, and that further enraged the white mob. Whites decided he was shot by a black worker named Daniel Wright, and a manhunt was launched.

Wright was tracked to his house, where white witnesses said he retreated to the attic and shot into the crowd, wounding two more white men.

The home was set afire and, with his wife watching, Wright was captured as he tried to escape. He was marched into the street and hit on the head with a pipe. A move was made to lynch him, but someone suggested he be given the chance to run for freedom. He ran about 50 yards before at least 40 guns opened fire on him. With 13 gunshot wounds, he clung to life at a hospital until the next morning, when he died.

A telegram came from Gov. Russell ordering the Wilmington Light Infantry under Col. Walker Taylor to preserve the peace. Meanwhile, the commander of the Naval Reserves tried unsuccessfully to find a city official to grant the military forces authority to take over. The governor ordered the Naval Reserve men to join Taylor's forces. They assembled at Third and Princess.

By noon, volleys were being fired throughout Brooklyn. Several black workers seeking to help friends were ordered to turn around and leave. They were shot at when they refused, with some dying on railroad tracks.

Forces of the WLI marched into Brooklyn, patrolling with a rapid-firing Colt gun mounted on a horse-drawn carriage. The Naval Reserves also wheeled a rapid-firing Hotchkiss gun through town.

Fighting broke out at Manhattan Park, with one man shot by members of the WLI on Bladen Street near Seventh Street.

One WLI private said the idea of shooting someone made him "sick to his stomach." He was told not to be a coward but to shoot. After the order to fire had come, it turned out the man had merely "snapped" his rifle. His cartridges lay on the ground beside him.

Telegrams went out to newspapers across the state and to President McKinley, who did not activate troops because he had not been asked to by Gov. Russell.

As the cold night fell, fearful black people hid in the woods or in outlying cemeteries.

One minister said "thousands of women, children and men rushed to the swamps and there lay upon the earth in the cold to freeze and starve." Others told similar stories.

Roads were lined with refugees leaving town, carrying personal belongings.

Democrats decided not to wait to take office at the end of the term of the sitting council, but demanded that the mayor, the police chief and members of the Board of Aldermen resign immediately. Waddell became the new mayor, leading an all-new, all-white board.

All black municipal employees were fired including city firefighters, a particular source of pride in the black community.

By the end of 1898, Wilmington was ruled by a purely Democratic regime and the purge was enlarged to include Fusionists in county government.

Celebrations were held in Wilmington and Raleigh. The Democratic Party printed a booklet called "North Carolina's Glorious Victory, 1898."

Leading blacks and some white Republicans were banished from Wilmington, some escorted at gunpoint to the train station. One man, Carter Peaman, was reportedly shot and killed when he tried to jump off the train. Families continued to stream out of the city.

Umfleet concludes that only a selected number of prominent white and black leaders were forced to leave. But thousands left in the days and weeks following the November 10 racial violence. Newspapers reported in December that more than 1,000 blacks had left.

Estimates of the number of people killed ranged from 10 to 20 to more than 100. Umfleet was able to compile a list of 22 people recorded as being killed, in some cases names unknown. But she says that "no accurate tally can be made" and that the list of documented deaths could reach as high as 60.

Democrats rewrote the city charter in 1899, repealing the Fusionist changes of 1895 and 1897 that had given the governor the power to appoint some local aldermen. It also gave the mayor power to force jobless "vagrants" to leave town or work on municipal projects.

The state legislature revised election laws to ensure Democratic victories in the 1900 elections. Red Shirts rode again, and the white supremacist orator Charles B. Aycock was elected governor. Republicans did not elect another candidate to statewide office for 70 years.

Starting in 1899, "Jim Crow" separate-but-equal laws were passed, the first of which segregated train compartments. In 1903, a local judge ruled that blacks and whites must use separate Bibles when being sworn to testify.

Blacks in Wilmington found themselves more at the mercy of white employers. Some upper-class families retained their property; Umfleet finds no instances where property was forcibly seized from black people and given to whites. But their children began moving away from Wilmington as tightening economic conditions resulted in the sale of black property to white buyers.

Many employers, encouraged by the Chamber of Commerce and newspapers, were firing blacks to hire whites.

The N.C. Office of Archives and History, working with the Institute of African-American Research at the University of North Carolina, looked at data from city directories in 1897 and 1900 to find economic trends.

By 1900, there were almost 1,000 fewer black workers in Wilmington. There were fewer skilled tradesmen but more laborers and industrial workers.

The number of black entrepreneurs in Wilmington fell 25 percent from 1897, while the number of white entrepreneurs fell just 2 percent.

Oddly, the number of black ministers grew from 13 to 40 in those three years, although the number of churches did not increase.

In 1897, black-owned businesses were located downtown and along North Fourth and South Seventh streets. By 1900, black entrepreneurship had become concentrated in black neighborhoods.

Conversely, by 1900, white-owned businesses began to fill downtown storefronts vacated by black businesses

The city became more segregated, with formerly mixed neighborhoods becoming predominately black or white.

Traditional "Jonnkonnu" or "Kunnering" celebrations, in which blacks would dress up and parade through neighborhoods at Christmas, came to an end in 1898 when Waddell's aldermen outlawed "the wearing of disguises of any kind."

It's not clear if the New Year's Day Emancipation Day observances were held in 1899 but they did resume in years following, although they were quieter and held only in the safety of black churches and schools.

The violence and coup in Wilmington became a blueprint for other white supremacy movements. Phoenix, S.C., also had a violent episode in 1898 in which at least 13 men were killed by white mobs.

At least six other incidents of racial violence followed in the next 25 years in which blacks lost lives, property and some of their rights. In 1906, violence in Atlanta left at least 25 blacks and two whites dead.

A 1921 riot in Tulsa, Okla., is probably the most violent racial clash in American history. The Tulsa police department deputized dozens of whites who murdered black citizens. Some 35 blocks in the black community were destroyed Estimates of the death toll ranged from 75 to 300.

As time passed in Wilmington, whites began to remember the 1898 coup as a necessary evil to end municipal corruption. Umfleet could find no evidence of that alleged corruption.

Black families passed down the memories, warning children to be wary of whites. As Wilmington's society grew more segregated, 1898 became an enduring example to black families of how far white society could go to achieve its ends.

Alex Manly's Editorial
August 18, 1898

A Mrs. Felton from Georgia, makes a speech before the Agricultural Society, at Tybee, Ga., in which she advocates lynching as an extreme measure. This woman makes a strong plea for womanhood and if the alleged crimes of rape were half so frequent as is oftimes reported, her plea would be worthy of consideration.

Mrs. Felton, like many other so-called Christians, loses sight of the basic principle of the religion of Christ in her plea for one class of people as against another. If a missionary spirit is essential for the uplifting of the poor white girls, why is it? The morals of the poor white people are on a par with their colored neighbors of like conditions and if one doubts that statement let him visit among them. The whole lump needs to be leavened by those who profess so much religion and showing them that the presence of virtue is an essential for the life of any people.

Mrs. Felton begins well for she admits that education will better protect the girls on the farm from the assaulter. This we admit and it should not be confined to the white any more than to the colored girls. The papers are filled often with reports of rapes of white women and the subsequent lynchings of the alleged rapists. The editors pour forth volumes of aspersions against all Negroes because of the few who may be guilty. If the papers and speakers of the other race would condemn the commission of the crime because it is crime and not try to make it appear that the Negroes were the only criminals, they would find their strongest allies in the intelligent Negroes themselves; and together the whites and blacks would root the evil out of both races.

We suggest that the whites guard their women more closely, as Mrs. Felton says, thus giving no opportunity for the human fiend, be he white or black. You leave your goods out of doors and then complain because they are taken away. Poor white men are careless in the matter of protecting their women, especially on the farms. They are careless of their conduct toward them and our experience teaches us that the women of that race are not any more particular in the matter of clandestine meetings with colored men than are the white men with colored women. Meetings of this kind go on for some time until the woman's infatuation, or the man's boldness, bring attention to them, and the man is lynched for rape. Every Negro lynched is called a "big burly, black brute," when in fact many of those who have thus been dealt with had white men for their fathers, and were not only not "black" and "burly" but were sufficiently attractive for white girls of culture and refinement to fall in love with them as is very well known to all.

Mrs. Felton must begin at the fountain head if she wishes to purify the stream.

Teach your men purity. Let virtue be something more than an excuse for them to intimidate and torture a helpless people. Tell your men that it is no worse for a black man to be intimate with a white woman than for the white man to be intimate with a colored woman.

You set yourselves down as a lot of carping hypocrites, in fact, you cry aloud for the virtue of your women while you seek to destroy the morality of ours. Don't ever think that your women will remain pure while you are debauching ours. You sow the seed–the harvest will come in due time.

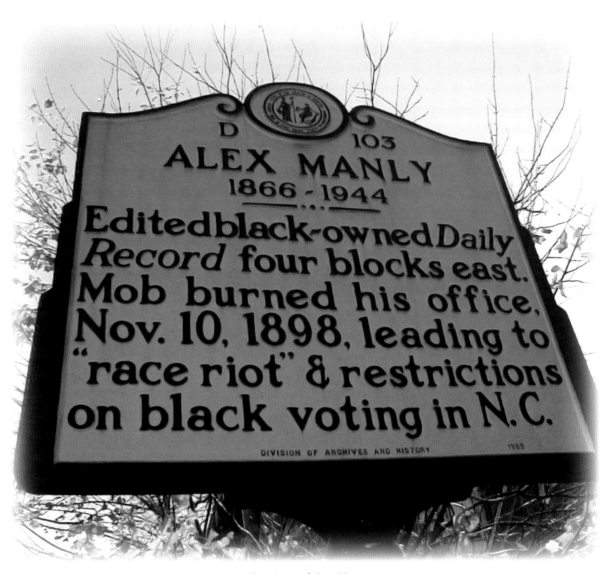

Courtesy of *Star News*

Researching the 1898 Race Riot
by Si Cantwell

LeRae Umfleet spent three years researching her report on the 1898 Race Riot.

She spent a lot of time in the North Carolina Room of the New Hanover County Public Library with history librarian Beverly Tetterton. She traveled to the University of North Carolina and Duke University, Livingstone College in Salisbury and elsewhere.

"I really just did some detective work," she said. Internet searches pointed her toward collections, some of which didn't always seem directly related to the subject. She read letters from husbands to wives to learn about events and gain a flavor of the times, and she performed what amounts to genealogy research to track down where victims lived and who they were.

She sometimes found it hard to distance herself from her studies.

"It got to me. I'm a mom," she said. "When the white men are marching to Manly's press building, they march past a schoolyard. The kids in the schoolyard are seeing white men with guns, and they're running to their moms and dads. It's scary."

She sympathized with the children who fled with their families after the riot, "going out into the woods," she said. "It was cold and sleeted

some. They only had the clothes they left home with, and maybe a blanket. It was scary seeing what happened to the children."

Umfleet is originally from Bath. She received her Masters degree from East Carolina University in 1998 after writing her thesis on "Slavery in Microcosm: Bertie County, North Carolina 1790-1810."

She joined the Department of Cultural Resources in 2003 as a research historian. She now serves as the department's chief of collections management.

Tetterton praised Umfleet's work.

"She impressed me because she left no stone unturned," Tetterton said. "The way she put the maps together; the ways she figured out what happened and where, and created the maps."

Tetterton, who oversees the county library's historic collections, had an additional observation that is chilling. She has looked at thousands of photographs of Wilmington over the years.

"Before 1898, you see African-Americans on the street. You see them walking and working," she said.

"After 1898, you don't see them as often. If a photograph is taken of a landmark building or an area of Wilmington, you don't see African-Americans on the street or standing at the building as much as you did in the 1870s, 1880s or 1890s," she said. "After the turn of the century, it was rare to see them."

Courtesy of *Star News*

Newspapers Acknowledge 1898 Role

by Si Cantwell

The 1898 Wilmington Race Riot Commission created by the General Assembly produced The 1898 Wilmington Race Riot Report, which was written by LeRae Umfleet of the state Office of Archives and History.

One of the 15 recommendations of the commission to "repair the moral, economic, civic and political damage wrought by the violence" was that newspapers "acknowledge the role of media in the events of 1898."

Toward that end, *The Charlotte Observer, The News & Observer of Raleigh* and the *Wilmington Star-News* cooperated in producing a special section looking back at 1898.

Its 11 chapters told the story of the events leading up to the race riot, the violence and the coup that replaced Wilmington's elected government, the banishment of successful black people and their white allies, and the aftermath and scars left by the events.

It was written by Timothy B. Tyson, senior research scholar at the Center for Documentary Studies at Duke University.

The *Star-News* published the section, titled "1898 Remembered: Wilmington's Race Riot and the Rise of White Supremacy," on November 17, 2006.

You can read it online at www.StarNewsOnline.com/1898.

Star-News
FRIDAY, NOVEMBER 17, 2006 | WILMINGTON, N.C.

1898 Remembered
WILMINGTON'S RACE RIOT AND THE RISE OF WHITE SUPREMACY

COURTESY OF N.C. OFFICE OF ARCHIVES & HISTORY

Destruction of 'The Daily Record' of Wilmington, said to be the only black-owned daily newspaper in the nation at the time, by white supremacists.

On Nov. 10, 1898, armed white men marched through the black sections of Wilmington, murdering all who dared to challenge them. As violence filled the streets, others snatched control of the government. After installing themselves in power, they banished at least 21 successful blacks and their white allies. Although it is one of the most significant chapters in the state history, it is a story many have never heard. In this special report, historian Timothy B. Tyson describes the carefully orchestrated campaign that spread white supremacy across North Carolina and the South. He explains how many of the region's leading figures and institutions seized power, altering the state's history and creating a legacy that haunts us still.

STORY BY TIMOTHY B. TYSON

The White Declaration of Independence

Printed in the Raleigh News and Observer, November 10, 1898

Believing that the Constitution of the United States contemplated a government to be carried on by an enlightened people; believing that its framers did not anticipate the enfranchisement of an ignorant population of African origin; and believing that the men of the State of North Carolina who joined in forming the Union did not contemplate for their descendants a subjection to an inferior race;

We, the undersigned citizens of the city of Wilmington and county of New Hanover, do hereby declare that we will no longer be ruled, and will never again be ruled, by men of African origin. This condition we have in part endured because we felt that the consequences of the war of secession were such to deprive us of the fair consideration of many of our countrymen. We believe that, after more than thirty years, this is no longer the case.

The stand we now pledge ourselves to is forced upon us suddenly by a crisis, and our eyes are open to the fact that we must act now or leave our descendants to a fate too gloomy to be borne.

While we recognize the authority of the United Sates and will yield to it if exerted, we would not for a moment believe that it is the purpose of more than 60,000,000 of our own race to subject us permanently to a fate to which no Anglo-Saxon has ever been forced to submit.

We, therefore, believing that we represent unequivocally the sentiment of the white people of this county and city, hereby for ourselves, and representing them, proclaim:

1. That the time has passed for the intelligent citizens of this community, owning 95 per cent of the property and paying taxes in like proportion, to be ruled by negroes.

2. That we will not tolerate the action of unscrupulous white men in affiliating with the negroes so that by means of their votes they can dominate the intelligent and thrifty element in the community, thus causing business to stagnate and progress to be out of the question.

3. That the negro has demonstrated, by antagonizing our interest in every way, and especially by his ballot, that he is incapable of realizing that his interests are and should be identical with those of the community.

4. That the progressive element in any community is the white population, and that the giving of nearly all of the employment to negro laborers has been against the best interests of this county and city, and is sufficient reason why the city of Wilmington with its natural advantages has not become a city of at least 50,000 inhabitants.

5. That we propose in the future to give the white men a large part of the employment heretofore given to negroes, because we realize that white families cannot thrive here unless there are more opportunities for the different members of said family.

6. That the white men expect to live in this community peaceably, to have and provide absolute protection for their families, who shall be safe from insult for all persons whomsoever. We are prepared to treat the negroes with justice and consideration in all matters which do not involve sacrifices of the interest of the intelligent and progressive portion of the community. But we are equally prepared now and immediately to enforce what we know to be our rights.

7. That we have been, in our desire for harmony and peace, blinded to our best interests and our rights. A climax was reached when the negro paper of this city published an article so vile and slanderous that it would in most communities have resulted in the lynching of the editor. We deprecate lynching, and yet there is no punishment provided by the laws adequate for this offense. We therefore owe it to the people of this community and of this city, as a protection against such license in the future, that the paper known as the *Record* cease to be published, and that its editor be banished from this community. We demand that he leave this city within twenty-four hours after the issuance of this proclamation; second, that the printing press from which the *Record* has been issued be packed and shipped from the city without delay; that we be notified within twelve hours of the acceptance or rejection of this demand. If it is agreed to within twelve hours, we counsel forbearance on the part of all white men. If the demand is refused, or if no answer is given within the time mentioned, then the editor, Manly, will be expelled by force.

8. It is the sense of this meeting that Mayor S.P. Wright and Chief of Police J.R. Melton, having demonstrated their utter incapacity to give the city a decent government and keep order therein, their continuance in office being a constant menace to the peace of this community, ought forthwith to resign.

The People's Declaration of Interdependence

Resolution adopted by the Executive Council of the 1898 Centennial Foundation on October 1, 1998 for submission to the citizens of Wilmington/New Hanover County on November 10, 1998, the centennial anniversary of the Wilmington coup of 1898.

Believing that the framers of the Constitution of the United States contemplated a government to be carried on by an enlightened people; believing that its principles fully anticipated the enfranchisement of human beings of all racial and ethnic origins; and believing that the people of the State of North Carolina who then and now join in forming the American Union do not wish for their descendants a division of society into a master and a servant relationship;

We, the undersigned citizens of the city of Wilmington and county of New Hanover, do hereby declare that we will no longer be ruled, and will never again be ruled, by the racist prejudices of the past, but instead we shall commit ourselves and the education of our children to the principle of racial equality and interdependence and the goal of racial harmony.

A direct consequence of the coup and violence of 1898 was a condition of injustice and oppression, which deprived many of our fellow citizens of their economic, social and political rights, and prolonged the insidious belief in white superiority. We believe that today, more than thirty years after the Civil Rights revolutions of the 1960's, this past must not only be acknowledged, but explicitly repudiated and reversed.

We, therefore, believing that we speak for the vast majority of today's citizens of this county and city, hereby proclaim:

1. The time has passed for the intelligent citizens of this community to be ruled by racism and prejudice.

2. We will no longer condone racist speech or behavior in our midst, neither by private individuals nor by public officials, and we will commit ourselves to a better future of racial equality and inclusion, for ourselves and our children.

3. A future of racial dialogue and interdependence is essential, if our community is to progress, morally and economically, in the 21st century.

4. The best interests of the community require the inclusion of African-Americans in all segments of the economy, particularly those from which they have been historically excluded, because African-American families cannot thrive in our community unless there are more opportunities for their economic advancement.

5. The best interests of the community require the inclusion of African-Americans in all segments of the political, judicial, and educational system, because democracy is not genuine, unless all groups and sectors of the society have a voice in the governance process.

6. People of all races expect to live in this community peaceably, to have and provide protection for their families, and to be safe from violence and from prejudice in the allocation of police resources.

7. We all know that the injustice that was inflicted on the African-Americans of Wilmington a century ago was wrong. We owe it to the people of this community, as a protection against such injustice in the future, to guarantee that the history of that past be an undeniable part of the public record, and we pledge ourselves to remove the vestiges of exclusion and segregation that were its bitter fruits.

8. All the political leaders of this city and county are called upon to declare openly their common commitment to the path of interracial dialogue, inclusion, and reconciliation without reservation.

Finally, it is the sense of this meeting that each and every political representative, business leader, and ordinary citizen should grasp this unique opportunity to commit themselves publicly to making WILMINGTON 1998 the diametrical opposite of WILMINGTON 1898 in race relations. Let this entire community become a shining beacon of racial equality and harmony, integrating all its social institutions and organizations; and positively fostering inclusion wherever exclusion has previously reigned. We are all well aware that it is the right thing to do and it is the right time to do it, so help us God.

Building a Firm Foundation

A diverse group of area citizens began meeting in November 1995 to share ideas about achieving a greater sense of community – leading to the formation of the Wilmington Alliance for Community Transformation (ACT). Described as a loosely knit advocacy organization, they held at least two public meetings during the spring of 1996. The first meeting was held April 24, 1996 at public radio station WHQR. The 35 participants broke into discussion groups. Four people of the eight who participated in a "Healing the Racial Wound" discussion—Bolton Anthony, Kenneth Davis, Francine DeCoursey and Aileen LeBlanc—would become actively involved in the 1898 commemorative effort.

Bolton Anthony applied for a grant from the North Carolina Humanities Council to fund ACT's second public meeting, two days of facilitated sessions with consultant Isaiah Madison, president of the Community Enterprise Development Foundation. A Howard University Law School graduate, Madison had previously served as executive director of the Institute for Southern Studies in Durham.

The planning grant outlined a series of events and initiatives to mark the centennial anniversary of Wilmington's coup of 1898, including: a city-wide program that promoted sensitivity to issues of cultural diversity and dialogue between the races, a 1998 residency by an historian, a radio drama, and the erection of a public monument to commemorate the event.

Each of these proposed activities would become part of the commemorative effort.

Meanwhile a group of UNCW faculty, including Melton McLaurin, Jack Manock, Earl Sheridan, and Phillip Gerard, had also begun exploring plans for a centennial observance. They had made preliminary contacts with approximately 15 community organizations. The two groups' slightly different agendas were incorporated into the planning for Madison's visit.

The visit concluded with a meeting at UNCW that was moderated by Melton McLaurin and attended by representatives of 30 community organizations. The foundation's organizational structure for the next six months—a loose association of representatives from community organizations—emerged from this meeting.

The meeting also resulted in a "clear consensus" that the group must "tell the story", "heal the wound", and "honor the memory." Based on the visit, Madison submitted a detailed report titled "The Racial Climate in Wilmington, North Carolina: June, 1996," which would become the essential planning document for the commemoration. He also emphasized the need for an economic development initiative and suggested that the commemoration's fourth tenet be "to restore the hope." Madison made subsequent trips to Wilmington to facilitate the planning process.

Bolton Anthony and William Fewell served as initial co-chairs of the effort, then called the 1898 Centennial Commission. When Fewell, an attorney and president of the local NAACP, returned to his Pennsylvania practice, Bertha Todd agreed to co-chair the effort.

As work began on incorporating the foundation, the group adopted the following mission statement and guiding principle:

Mission Statement

Our mission is to develop and coordinate a broad-based community effort in appropriate remembrance of the Wilmington coup and violence of 1898.

It is our hope that this remembrance will be the beginning of a continuing effort to improve race relations in Wilmington and help bring about a spirit of justice and tolerance for all residents of the community.

Guiding Principle

The Foundation will strive to overcome institutional racism by providing for co-chair positions of the Foundation and its committees. Other diversities will be considered as well. The By-Laws will provide a mechanism to solve incidents of impasse. By joining this organization members accept a personal commitment to free themselves of any prejudices or antagonisms based on race and to act in conformity with this principle and toward this goal.

Recognizing the organization's mission and activities could extend beyond the 1998, the group applied for its status as a non-profit organization as the 1898 Foundation, Inc. The request was approved on September 24, 1997. Prior to receiving the IRS designation, the North Fourth Street Partnership, of which Anthony served as executive director, served as fiscal agent for the project.

With a $25,000 grant from the Z. Smith Reynolds Foundation, the organization was able to hire a for a half-time executive secretary. Roberta Troy was appointed to the position in mid-February. When she resigned a month later, the position was split into two part-time positions; and Rhonda Bellamy and Becky Long were hired. Funding in the amount of $5,000 was also approved by Wilmington City Council.

Bolton Anthony
Man on a Mission
by Rhonda Bellamy

He has a knack for landing in peculiar places at peculiar times. Bolton Anthony doesn't really know why he came to Wilmington. Perhaps it was the lure of a job at UNCW managing a grant on race relations. The *hardest* job would take the next five years as first co-chair of the 1898 Centennial Commission and later executive director of the 1898 Foundation.

"A year into the UNCW project, my mother sent me the history of a small Episcopal parish in Thibodeaux, Mississippi – Cajun country. In the history, which gave short bios of elders who had helped establish the church, was my great-great grandfather, Richard Ray Darden. He was born in Wilmington in 1805, moved to Louisiana in 1836, and had slaves on his sugar plantation, said Anthony.

"Am I working out karma for my relatives?" he mused, reflecting on a common thread throughout his professional life. His first teaching job was at Xavier University, a black university in New Orleans, the year Dr. Martin Luther King, Jr. was killed.

After arriving in Wilmington, "it didn't take much more than five or six conversations to identify that 1898 was an undercurrent in race relations," said Anthony. The late Lisbon Berry, a prominent attorney, was clearest about the need for a commemoration, he added.

"In November, 1995, a small diverse group... including educators, business owners and health care providers began meeting informally to share their ideas and hopes for greater connectedness, meaning and future opportunity within their community," Anthony wrote in Confronting 1898, a complete record of the centennial commemoration.

From these meetings a loosely knit "advocacy organization" — The Wilmington Alliance for Community Transformation (ACT) — emerged. ACT held at least two public meetings during the spring of 1996. At its first meeting, held April 24, 1996 in the community room of public radio station WHQR, the approximately 35 participants broke into discussion groups. The focus of one of those groups was "Healing the Racial Wound."

Anthony was one of eight participants in that discussion. Others included Kenneth Davis, Francine DeCoursey and Aileen LeBlanc— all of whom would become actively involved in the commemorative effort. By year's end, the 1898 Centennial Commission was formed.

Anthony and William Fewell, an attorney and president of the local NAACP chapter, served as initial co-chairs of the effort. When Fewell returned to his Pennsylvania law practice, Bertha Todd accepted the co-chairmanship.

"He was low-key," Todd said of Anthony, "but little by little, he was getting together groups of individuals in the community to uncover just what happened in 1898 and work towards a commemoration."

"Bertha Todd brought a repertoire of skills and a range of contacts, in both the white and black community, that proved critical to the success of the effort. She also set a tone for the effort which allowed bridges to be built with the political and business communities. The phrase "Moving Forward Together" (which became the title of the Opening Ceremony in January 1998) was a watchword for Bertha," Anthony wrote.

He credits Todd's positive approach to overcoming unfounded fears that the commemoration could "get out of hand."

The 1898 effort is not the only large-scale project Anthony has undertaken. While working with the public library in Fayetteville, NC, he developed a series of public humanities projects that culminated in "The Unimagined City," a 13-week residency by the founding dean of the School of Design at North Carolina State. That project led directly to a citizen action committee and — seven years later — to the "Fayetteville Renaissance," chronicled in a 1985 Smithsonian World documentary. In 1980, Anthony was made an honorary citizen of Fayetteville.

Born in New Orleans and raised in Houston, Anthony has an undergraduate degree from the University of Notre Dame; his three graduate degrees include an Ed.D. in Educational Administration from the University of North Carolina at Greensboro.

He is now founder and president of Second Journey, a non-profit to promote "mindfulness, service and community in the second half of life." *His* second journey includes life with wife Lisa in Chapel Hill, NC.

On a visit to Wilmington shortly after installation of the major sculptural elements of the 1898 Memorial Park, Bolton said his first impression was "Wow, that was worth it!"

1996-2008

1898 Centennial Foundation
1898 Foundation Executive Council Members

Vivian Alexander

Bolton Anthony, 1898 Foundation Founding Co-chair, 1898 Foundation Executive Director

Dianne Avery, Education Committee Co-chair

Rhonda Bellamy, 1898 Foundation Co-Executive Secretary/Staff, Drama Committee Chair, Editor, *Moving Forward Together*

Kathleen Berkeley, 1898 Foundation Historian

Shirley Hart Berry, 1898 Foundation Executive Council Secretary

Jan Broadfoot, Banquet Artist Coordination Committee Chair

Tandy Carter, Appointed by Wilmington City Council

John Cease, Appointed by Wilmington City Council

William "Bill" Childs (late), Reconciliation Committee Co-chair, Banquet Awards Committee Chair

Sue Cody, Educational Committee Co-chair

Margaret Craig, Staff

William Crawford

Windell Daniels (late), Appointed by Greater Wilmington Chamber of Commerce, Banquet Fundraising Committee Chair

Kenneth Davis, 1898 Foundation Historian, Education Committee Co-chair, Heritage Tourism Committee Co-chair, 1898 Foundation Executive Council Secretary

Francine DeCoursey, Education Committee Co-chair, Documentary Producer

Inez Campbell Eason, Memorial Committee Co-chair

Daawuud El-Amin

William Fewell, 1898 Foundation Executive Council Founding Co-chair

Lethetta Forbes

Terry Gandy

Rob Gerlach, Appointed by Greater Wilmington Chamber of Commerce, Economic Development Co-chair, Partners for Economic Inclusion Committee Co-chair, 1898 Foundation Executive Council Co-chair

Peter Grear, Economic Development Committee Co-chair, Partners for Economic Inclusion Committee Co-chair

John Haley, 1898 Foundation Historian

Lethia Hankins, 1898 Foundation Executive Council Co-chair, Memorial Campaign Committee Co-chair

Herbert Harris, Jr., 1898 Foundation Executive Council Co-chair

The Rev. June Highfill, Ministerial Roundtable Co-chair

W. K. Hobbs, Jr., Appointed by Greater Wilmington Chamber of Commerce

Leslie Hossfeld, Program Committee Co-chair

Paul Jefferson, 1898 Book Committee

Harvard Jennings, Memorial Committee Co-chair

Minister Ali Kaazim

Aileen LeBlanc, Memorial Committee Co-chair

Helena Lee, Education Committee Co-chair

Becky Long, 1898 Foundation Executive Council Secretary, 1898 Foundation Co-Executive Secretary/Staff, Operations Committee Co-chair

Rose Ann Mack, Appointed by Wilmington City Council

Linda MacRae, Program Committee Co-chair

Jack Manock, Appointed by New Hanover County Commissioners, Foundation Committee Co-chair, Economic Development Committee Co-chair

Fred McCree (late)

Alfredia McDonald

Herb McKim

Melton McLaurin, 1898 Foundation Historian, 1898 Foundation Executive Council Co-chair, Memorial Campaign Committee Co-chair

James Megivern, 1898 Foundation Executive Council Co-chair

Marjorie Megivern

Rosalind Mosley, 1898 Foundation Executive Council Secretary

Mary Elizabeth Nixon

Laura W. Padgett, Appointed by Wilmington City Council, 1898 Foundation Executive Council Co-chair, Memorial Committee Co-chair

Yvonne Pagan

Ginny Peterson, Banquet Publicity Committee Chair

Harper Peterson, Appointed by Wilmington City Council

Nelson Robinson

Margaret Rogers, 1898 Foundation Historian, 1898 Foundation Executive Council Secretary

Tom Schmid, 1898 Foundation Executive Council Co-chair, Program Committee Co-chair

Earl Sheridan, Operations Committee Co-chair, Education Committee Co-chair

Derrick Sherman

Linda Upperman Smith, 1898 Foundation Executive Council Co-chair, Banquet Committee Chair

Trish Snyder, Reconciliation Committee Co-chair

Rhonda Stevens

Barbara Sullivan, 1898 Foundation Executive Council Co-chair, Reconciliation Committee Vice-chair

Sherma Svitzer, Program Committee Co-chair

Hunter Thompson

Bertha Todd, 1898 Foundation Executive Council Co-chair, Memorial Committee Co-chair

Hannah Vaughan

Ruchadina Waddell

Anthony Wade, Appointed by New Hanover County Commissioners

Harry Warren

Charlie West, 1898 Foundation Executive Council Treasurer

Bertha Williams

Ethan Williamson, Program Committee Co-chair

Lloyd Wilson, Memorial Selection Panel

The Rev. Dr. Joseph Windley (late) - Appointed by New Hanover County Commissioners

Statement on Reparations

It has been documented that during the Wilmington coup and violence of 1898, in addition to the loss of life, many African-Americans had their livelihoods and property unjustly taken away. The acknowledgment of harsh realities such as these is a crucial aspect of the healing, which we hope will come out of the commemoration of that event. It is our position, however, that the actual seeking of reparations or other redress for individual acts of confiscation is something best left to the descendants of those whose property was taken. Our task with the 1898 Foundation will be the larger task of bringing to the light of day what transpired, commemorating the event, helping to create an atmosphere conducive to equal opportunity and empowerment and in so doing bring about reconciliation. A key component of that reconciliation is gaining economic development for the African-American community as a whole because the black community as a whole, not just the direct descendants of victims, has been adversely affected and its economic growth stunted by the events of 1898.

Meg Mulrooney's "Official" History

In the spring of 1997, the foundation contracted with Dr. Margaret Mulrooney of the history department at UNCW to produce a condensed history of the 1898 racial violence that was published by the Foundation in its next three quarterly newsletters. Mulrooney also produced an extended essay, which was particularly useful in raising economic perspectives and placing the event in a broader national and regional context.

Major Initiatives

Forum Features Grandson of Ousted Alderman

The first public forum sponsored by the 1898 Centennial Commission was held at Cape Fear Museum on Sunday, November 10, 1996, the 98th anniversary of the coup. An estimated 180 people attended the forum, which featured UNCW history professor John Haley, who discussed the coup and its broader historical context. Local actress Dale Wright performed a dramatic reading of a poignant letter written to President McKinley six days after the rioting by a black woman who urged federal intervention. The program concluded with remarks from Thomas Keith, a district attorney from Winston-Salem who was the grandson of B.F. Keith, an elected alderman who was deposed during the 1898 coup and who was among a delegation that tried unsuccessfully to meet with President McKinley in Washington.

A Handshaking Across Troubled Waters

The 1921 race riots in Tulsa, Oklahoma bore similar consequences as the 1898 racial violence in Wilmington. The Tulsa incident resulted in the deaths of hundreds of blacks and the decimation of the prosperous business district known as "Black Wall Street."

Oklahoma State Representative Don Ross and Tulsa Mayor Susan Savage, who were instrumental in commemorating the 75th anniversary of the tragedy, shared their experience during a March 14-15, 2007 visit to Wilmington.

Both emphasized the need to involve the ministerial community and the political leadership in the effort. Ross also offered specific information about heritage tourism, which the foundation's economic development committee would later pursue.

"If a commemoration is anything," said Ross, "it's getting to know one another. It's a handshaking across troubled waters."

Their presentations to Wilmington citizens, elected officials, historians, and religious leaders were recorded on videotape and later edited for use with community groups.

The Tulsa incident was sparked when a 19-year-old black man named Dick Rowland got on an elevator in a Tulsa office building to find a bathroom open to him under the state's Jim Crow laws. In the elevator, he stepped on the foot of a 17-year-old white female elevator operator. She slapped Rowland, who fled the elevator. Word first spread that he had assaulted woman; by evening, she was alleged to have been raped.

While Rowland was jailed at the Tulsa County courthouse, shots were fired between a white mob who had gathered after hearing the inflammatory news accounts and blacks who gathered to protect Roland from lynching as suggested by the local newspaper. Tulsa police deputized and armed hundreds of white men and boys who traveled into Greenwood, where some joined a mob in shooting at residents and setting fire to black-owned businesses and residences. When the Oklahoma National Guard was called in to restore order, troops disarmed blacks and took thousands of African-American residents into "protective custody" by mass arrest, leaving the neighborhood unprotected. Twenty-two square blocks—1,256 homes and virtually every other structure, including a library and hospital, churches and schools—lay in ashes the next day. A 2001 commission report concluded that it was impossible to determine the number of people killed in the riot. The case against Rowland was later dismissed.

"Understanding 1898: A Seminar for Clergy."

As part of its Reconciliation Committee, the foundation created a Ministerial Roundtable, led then by the Rev. Joe Cooper (Church of the Servant), Rabbi Robert Waxman (B'Nai Israel Synagogue), the Rev. Lone Jensen (Unitarian Universalist Fellowship of Wilmington) and the Rev. Joseph Windley (First Baptist Church).

In what was described as the largest gathering of Wilmington clergy in many years, the seminar on May 30, 1997 drew over 50 people representing more than 22 different faiths. Dr. John Haley provided an historical overview, and Susan King and Dale Wright collaborated on dramatic readings of letters written by a black and a white citizen in 1898. Remarks by Dr. Jim Megivern of the UNCW Department of Philosophy and Religion preceded a general discussion, which was facilitated by Harvard Jennings.

Wilmington in Black and White

A weekly series of ten programs, titled Wilmington in Black and White, examined "the Wilmington experience"—"its history, churches, schools, businesses, arts, architecture, and community relations. The series was moderated by Dr. Jim Megivern, a member of the Executive Council (who would later replace Anthony as co-chair), and a faculty member in the Department of Philosophy and Religion at UNCW, Each program featured two presenters, one black, the other white. The first series ran September 18–November 20, 1997 at UNCW and was free and open to the public. Most of the programs were videotaped; and these were rebroadcast several times during 1998.

The enthusiastic response to the series encouraged Megivern to "rerun" it—this time, however, at St. Stephen A.M.E. Church in downtown Wilmington. The number of programs was reduced to eight, and there were shifts among the speakers. The high point of the series was its second session, "Different Perspectives on the Causes of Events of 1898." This February 5, 2008 program featured Dr. John Haley and George Rountree, III.

Interfaith Candlelight Vigil

On the eve of the 99th anniversary of the coup of 1898, over 100 people gathered at Riverfront Park at sunset for an interfaith candlelight vigil. Local clergy and others led participants in a program of readings and prayers for spiritual guidance and direction for our community as we began a year dedicated to reflection, remembrance, and racial reconciliation. The November 9, 1997 service concluded with the lighting of a flame, which was then passed from candle to candle as the group repeated the words "...we forgive ourselves and each other, we begin again in love."

"Remembering 1898" — An Introductory Video.

Local filmmaker and Executive Council member Francine DeCoursey produced and directed a 23-minute video featuring an historical overview by UNCW professors John Haley, Meg Mulrooney, and Melton McLaurin. Additional remarks about the importance of the commemoration were made by Bessie Funderburg, Jim Megivern, Rev. Joseph Windley, Bertha Todd, Bolton Anthony and Kenneth Davis. Two other videos would follow, including one of the visit of Oklahoma State Representative Don Ross and Tulsa Mayor Susan Savage. In the third video local actresses Dale Wright and Susan King read from actual letters written in 1898. In the spring of 1998, Governor James Hunt recorded an introductory message, which was appended to the beginning of the video.

DeCoursey also shot raw documentary footage on other key activities including: the January 17 Opening Ceremony at Brogden Hall, footage from the Azalea Festival parade, the July 15 program at Screen Gems, the "Conversation Among Descendants," recorded after the UNCW symposium, the Friday evening performance of "No More Sorrow to Arise" and the reception, the November 10 Commemorative Ceremony and the reception, and the November 14 Centennial Foundation Banquet.

African-American History Series

A series of four Sunday afternoon programs focusing on the achievements of African-Americans living in Wilmington was held October 19-November 16, 1997. The years 1857, 1877, 1897 and 1919 served as benchmarks for the programs. At each session, an academic historian discussed the broad regional and historical context, and local historian Margaret Rogers provided background on the local situation.

The first program, held at Bellamy Mansion on October 5, 1997, featured Dr. John David Smith, professor of history and director of the Public History Program at North Carolina State University. His focus was on the antebellum period, circa 1857, when skilled African-American laborers built structures such as the Bellamy Mansion. The slave quarter on the site illustrated the living conditions of urban African-Americans circa 1857.

The second program focused on the Reconstruction period and featured Dr. David Cecelski, historian at the Southern Oral History Program at the University of North Carolina at Chapel Hill. His research focused on Abraham H. Galloway, an escaped slave, Union spy and soldier, and state senator. The program was held at Saint Mark's Episcopal Church, built in 1871.

The third program examined the pinnacle of nineteenth century African-American political and economic achievement, including the elections of 1896 and 1897. Due to illness, Dr. Beverly Jones, professor of history and director of the Institute of Minority Issues at North Carolina Central University, was unable to participate in the November 2, 1997 session at the historic New Hanover Courthouse, completed in 1892. Dr. John Haley agreed to serve in her place.

Dr. John Haley, associate professor of history at UNCW, discussed African-American experiences during and after World War I. Returning to a Jim Crow Wilmington in economic decline presented difficult challenges to African-American soldiers who had traveled the U.S. and Europe. The final program was held November 16, 1997 at Cape Fear Museum.

The series was a collaboration with the Bellamy Mansion Museum and Cape Fear Museum.

The African-American Heritage Trail

The inaugural tour of the African-American Heritage Trail was held October 11, 1997. Five of the 17 sites featured in the brochure "Wilmington, North Carolina's African-American Heritage Trail" were visited. The tour ended at Cape Fear Museum where Dr. Meg Mulrooney and the students from her public history class talked to a large enthusiastic group about the research project that had helped create the brochure.

The sites included on the Heritage Trail were:

Wilmington, North Carolina's
AFRICAN AMERICAN HERITAGE TRAIL

Cape Fear Museum

Bellamy Mansion Museum of History and Design Arts/Bellamy Mansion Slave Quarters

City Hall/Thalian Hall

Wilmington National Cemetery

Chestnut Street Presbyterian Church

Williston Academy, Gregory Normal Institute, and Gregory Congregational United Church of Christ

Pine Forest Cemetery

St. Mark's Episcopal Church

Giblem Lodge

Sadgwar Family House (Baha'i Center)

The Wilmington *Daily Record* and the *Wilmington Journal*

John Taylor House/Wilmington Light Infantry Armory

Brooklyn (4th & Harnett Sts.)

Business District (Red Cross Street and adjacent area bounded by N. Fifth, Campbell, N. Seventh, and Walnut Sts.

Williston Industrial High School and Williston Senior High School

St. John's Museum of Art

New Hanover High School

Moving Forward Together

"Programs such as yours help us to focus on the things that unite rather than divide us. I commend all of you for helping us to recognize anew that working together in a spirit of community is not a hope but a necessity, that our individual dreams can only be realized by our common efforts."

President Bill Clinton

More than 600 people attended the "Opening Ceremony" on January 17, 1998, at Brogden Hall. The event kicked off centennial year activities, including a dialogue series on race.

Remarks from President Clinton, read by U.S. Representative Mike McIntyre, commended the community on its effort "to find the common ground of cooperation."

The Rev. Doug Tanner, executive director of the Faith and Politics Institute in Washington and the founder of Common Ground, served as the keynote speaker. Other speakers included Representative Eva Clayton and Eddie Lawrence, director of the North Carolina Human Relations Commission, who spoke on behalf of the governor. Wilmington Mayor Hamilton Hicks and New Hanover County Commissioner Bill Caster also spoke.

Public attendance at the Opening Ceremony was helped by two events. The program coincided with the public opening of a well-publicized exhibit that chronicled the 100-year history of the Cape Fear Museum (whose centennial anniversary also occurred in 1998). Both these events occurred on the Saturday of the Martin Luther King weekend. Three days earlier, Martin Luther King III, in another well-publicized event, had urged a packed auditorium "at UNCW to take action and keep hope alive." King was aware of the "tragic incident" and in his remarks expressed hope that the commemoration "will bring the community together and not divide" it.

The program included performances by storyteller/musician Lloyd Wilson, Wilmington percussionists and performers led by Peter Zukoski, the combined voices of the Wilmington Girls and Boys choirs, and the UNCW Gospel Choir. Church Women United presented a parade of banners and the YWCA of Wilmington conducted the closing ceremony where all those present waved lights in the darkened auditorium and sang "Let There Be Peace On Earth."

Launch of Study Circles

"If we're really going to learn anything from each other, we really need to spend a little bit of time just hanging out—being with each other as friends. That's happening because as these dialogue groups conclude, relationships are continuing. People are coming back together."

Reconciliation Committee member Peggy Schroeder

Wilmington was designated as one of 55 host cities for the National Days of Dialogue on Race Relations, prompting inquiries from the national media, including the *Los Angeles Times* and NBC News.

The foundation's Reconciliation Committee set a goal of recruiting and training 100 facilitators to produce 50 racially balanced teams. Sarah Campbell, the director of Study Circles, directed the training sessions, which were held on November 21–22, 1997. Teams of black and white facilitators met with small groups of 10-15 participants in five two-hour sessions. These dialogue groups gave participants the opportunity to explore the issue of race. Reading materials provided structure for the dialogues, and trained facilitators helped ensure lively but focused discussions.

Study Circles was a generic program aimed at fostering interracial dialogue. The program was customized by adding a session on "Dealing with 1898." Dr. Thomas Schmid, a professor in the Department of Philosophy and Religion at UNCW and a member of the committee, prepared a PowerPoint presentation, "The Revolution of 1898" that was useful in developing the guidelines for facilitating the new session.

Trish Snyder reported on February 10 that 400 people had signed up for the community dialogues. At the April meeting of the Executive Council, Barbara Sullivan reported that 131 black and 219 white citizens had signed up for the community dialogues. Not all individuals had been placed at this time, but the first group, facilitated by Wallace Murchison and Connie O'Dell, had begun.

An "Authentic Experience" with Caletha Powell

The foundation's Economic Development Committee settled on heritage tourism as an initiative that would serve as a "living memorial." A consulting visit by Caletha Powell, director of the National Institute for Tourism Research and Training, was held April 29–May 2, 1998.

A past president of the New Orleans Visitor's Information Center and appointed by the late Secretary Ron Brown to serve on the U.S. Travel and Tourism Advisory Board, she was serving a third term on the Board of Directors of the Travel Industry Association of America. A native of North Carolina, she had worked in development at Fayetteville State University, her alma mater, and chaired the NC Council on the Status of Women.

Powell's visit included a reception with local tourism and travel industry representatives, public officials and business leaders. She discussed how other communities and states were capitalizing on the fastest growing segment of the industry – heritage-based tourism.

She "inventoried Wilmington's assets" during a bus tour of North Fourth Street and other inner city historic sites as well as the Seabreeze community. A boat excursion up the Cape Fear River visited Pocomoke, an isolated African-American settlement whose historical roots date back to the mid-1700's. On Saturday morning Powell shared her preliminary recommendations with the community.

- Advocate for a statewide initiative — with Wilmington as its anchor — that will utilize heritage tourism development as a strategy for creating jobs and minority-owned businesses.

- Develop your "asset base" through research on significant people, places and events related to the African-American heritage and culture of the state and position Wilmington as a state and national model for heritage tourism development.

- Establish a non-profit organization within the black community to implement local initiatives. Working in collaboration with the 1898 Centennial Foundation, the non-profit would push the development of African-American heritage sites and press for their inclusion in the overall tourism product of the city.

- Link revitalization efforts in the historic areas of North Fourth and Castle Streets to initiatives that interpret the history of 1898. This would include new initiatives such as historical tours, an 1898 memorial, and an outdoor drama performed in the proposed Castle Street amphitheater. The feasibility of converting Holy Trinity Church to a state museum, as part of a major educational and economic development strategy, should also be explored.

- Restore the Seabreeze area as an historic site, obtaining a designation on the National Register of Historic Places.

- Preserve the entire Pocomoke area as an historic district, maintaining the natural environmental and cultural character of the area, and create economic development opportunities, such as boat tours.

Powell visited Wilmington again in July, when she spoke at the event at Screen Gems. During that stay, she also visited Atlanta Beach, SC, a historically black beach area north of Myrtle Beach, to follow-up on conversations with the town mayor about regional collaboration.

During the summer and fall, the Economic Development Committee took some initial steps to implement Powell's recommendations. Articles of Incorporation were filed for the Carolinas Heritage Tourism Network, the black-controlled non-profit that Powell had argued was needed to insure the economic pay-off to the black community in new business ownership opportunities and job creation.

photo by Daniel Ray Norris

Prominent Historians Headline UNCW Symposium

by Rhonda Bellamy

Courtesy of *Star News*

"Perhaps some day in the near or distant future, place will have for African-Americans the same meaning it has for other Americans."

Dr. John Hope Franklin

Racial violence in 1898 Wilmington was neither random nor isolated. "Violence seemed to be a way of life in the South in that period," said Dr. John Hope Franklin.

The Duke University professor emeritus and author of the definitive book *From Slavery to Freedom* was the keynote speaker at the 1898 Wilmington Racial Violence and its Legacy symposium. More than a thousand people attended the two-day event, October 23-24, 1998, at UNCW.

The symposium opened with the unveiling of a new state highway historical marker by UNCW Chancellor James Leutze, Secretary of Cultural Resources Betty McCain, and Wilmington Mayor Hamilton Hicks honoring black newspaperman Alexander Manly, whose *Daily Record* was burned to the ground in 1898.

"People don't usually burn houses down – burn the newspaper down – just because they disagreed with the newspaper," Franklin said at a news conference.

Rather some whites believed that because of the new freedoms enjoyed by an increasingly prosperous and majority black population, blacks had forgotten their place.

"If Wilmington brought the 19th century to an inglorious end, violence in other cities would soon help usher in the 20th," he said of violence that broke out in Louisiana, Georgia, Chicago, and his native Tulsa, Oklahoma.

Franklin's remarks came just weeks after he delivered a report as chairman of President Bill Clinton's advisory panel on race relations.

Other speakers included co-editors David S. Cecelski and Timothy B. Tyson of *Democracy Betrayed*, as well as professors William Chafe, Duke University; Glenda Gilmore, Yale University; Leon Prather, Tennessee State University; LeAnn Whites, University of Missouri-Columbia; John Haley UNC-Wilmington; Beverly Washington Jones, N.C. Central University; and others.

The symposium was attended by a number of descendants living in other parts of the country. The 1898 Foundation used the opportunity to videotape "A Conversation among Descendants," which was recorded following the conclusion of the symposium. Participants included Frankye Manly Jones, the niece of Alex Manly, and Ida Manly, the daughter-in-law of Frank Manly; Laurie Gunst, the granddaughter of former Wilmington mayor Salomon Fishblatte; Bill Collins, a Burnett family descendant; Richard Yarborough from UCLA, one of the symposium speakers; and Cynthia Brown and Inez Eason of Wilmington.

Dr. Melton McLaurin at UNCW and Jeffrey Crowe, director of the Division of Archives and History, co-chaired the planning for the symposium, which was sponsored by their respective institutions, in association with the North Carolina Literary and Historical Association.

Publication of the symposium's proceedings, *Democracy Betrayed*, was edited by David Cecelski and Timothy Tyson.

"Those who resist change are reminiscent of the ex-Confederates who, in the years following the Civil War, preferred to dream of a South that never was and never could be rather than accept one that was within the reach of all, if they would join together and make it so," wrote Franklin in the book's foreword.

Descendant Cynthia Brown
Courtesy of *Star News*

Historian David S. Cecelski, Co-editor, *Democracy Betrayed*
Courtesy of *Star News*

photo by Daniel Ray Norris

1898 Commendations

Cultural Diversity Award - National League of Cities
Cape Fear Peace Prize - Dispute Settlement Center of the Cape Fear
Organization of the Year - New Hanover Co. Human Relations Commission
The Universal Fellowship of Metropolitan Community Churches
The Bahá'ís of Wilmington

November 1998
Commemorative Ceremony

Thalian Hall was the setting for two events one hundred years and worlds apart. Vastly different scenarios played out in a venue where citizens in 1898 would overthrow a government and citizens in 1998 would overthrow racial reservations.

In the culmination of a year of public activities, over 500 people – black and white, young and old – gathered on November 10, 1998. As the sounds of Pamoja! faded, the introduction was delivered offstage by 1898 co-chair Bertha Todd. A "Litany in Remembrance of the Events of 1898," composed by Rev. Lone Jensen, was read by 1898 Ministerial Roundtable co-chairs, Rev. Johnny Calhoun and Rev. June Highfill. School children read their poems about 1898. The combined choirs of St. Luke AME Zion Church and First Presbyterian Church, led by Marva Robinson and Doug Leightenheimer, shared inspirational performances of "Amazing Grace," "Let There Be Peace On Earth," I've Been 'buked," and "The Battle Hymn of the Republic."

Past and present slides of Wilmington appeared intermittently on a giant screen — the final slide of two children, one black, one white, summed up the commemoration: hope for the future.

In a fitting end to the program, the audience joined in reading the "Peoples' Declaration of Racial Interdependence." This document was written by members of the Reconciliation Committee in rebuttal to the "White Declaration of Independence," a white supremacy document which had been read at Thalian Hall one hundred years earlier and had been signed by over 400 Wilmingtonians. Though the lines were long and slow, those in attendance in 1998 waited to sign the historic new document.

Commemorative Banquet

"After 100 years Wilmington has confronted its 'dangerous memory'," Bolton Anthony said in remarks at the 1898 Commemorative Banquet November 14, 1998. The focus must shift now to "the challenge of creating the future for Wilmington that all persons of good will desire."

While the commemoration had helped launch important initiatives, proceeds from the banquet would fund continued work on heritage-based tourism and the establishment of a permanent monument.

The keynote speaker was Ben Ruffin, who had just been elected president of the Board of Governors of the University of North Carolina system—the first black to hold that position. In a surprise gesture, Kenneth Davis and Bolton Anthony were honored with plaques recognizing their contributions to the commemorative effort.

An ad hoc committee, chaired by Linda Upperman Smith, managed the event's details, including exhibiting artists and booksellers.

The banquet brought a conclusion to the public activities of the centennial Commemoration.

Other Events and Programs

January 17, 1998
Looking Back: Cape Fear Museum's First 100 Years
Public Opening of Exhibit

January 31, 1998
Eracism: A Discussion of Race
A play presented by the Dispute Settlement Center of Cape Fear, Inc to demonstrate the management of inter-racial conflict.

March 20, 1998
"Let My People Go"
A drama by the Touring Theatre Ensemble of North Carolina based on recently collected court documents, compiled and edited by University of North Carolina at Greensboro history professor Loren Schweninger.

March 30, 1998
Public Forum on the Memorial

April 4, 1998
Azalea Festival Parade

July 15, 1998
Remembering 1898: A Corporate Overview
Wes Beckner, president of the Greater Wilmington Chamber of Commerce, and Gerry McCants, president of the Black Chamber of Commerce briefed corporate leaders about the centennial commemoration in an event hosted by Frank Capra, Jr. at Screen Gems Studios.

August 6, 1998
Alex Manly: Truth and Speculation
Dr. Bob Wooley discussed newspaperman Alex Manly at Cape Fear Museum. Wooley, who is a professor of history at Mansfield University in Pennsylvania, has been a student of Manly for over 20 years.

September 2, 1998
Partners for Economic Inclusion Conference
The inaugural activity of a coalition comprised of representatives from the Greater Wilmington Chamber of Commerce, the Black Chamber of Commerce and the 1898 Economic Development Committee. Walter McDowell, president and CEO of Wachovia Bank, was conference keynote speaker.

September 19, 1998
Publication of "Strength Through Struggle"
The New Hanover County Public Library hosted a reception celebrating the publication of *Strength Through Struggle: The Chronological and Historical Record of the African-American Community in Wilmington, North Carolina, 1865-1950*. This comprehensive local history was compiled by Bill Reaves from local newspaper reports and edited by local history librarian Beverly Tetterton

September 24, 1998
The Wilmington Riot of 1898 in Fiction
The New Hanover County Public Library presented Wilmington native Anita D. Haynes, who is a librarian in Las Vegas, Nevada. She discussed the novels *The Marrow of Tradition*, by Charles Chesnutt, *Hanover*, by Thorne, and *Cape Fear Rising*, by Philip Gerard. Sponsored by the New Hanover County Public Library.

September 26-27, 1998
David Walker Festival
The Friends of David Walker, Inc. hosted the 10th Annual "Family Day Multi-Cultural Festival." This annual event honored the legacy of native son, David Walker, author of *David Walker's Appeal*.

October 15-16, 1998
No More Secrets
Celia Bland, author of the children's book *The Conspiracy of the Secret Nine*, discussed the events surrounding 1898 with middle school students and Wilmington residents. A public reading and book signing were also held. Ms. Bland was accompanied by Rhonda Bellamy, who read excerpts from the book. Sponsored by Cape Fear Museum, in conjunction with New Hanover County Schools and Barnes & Noble Booksellers.

October 18, 1998
1898: The Riots
UNCW historians Melton McLaurin and John Haley discussed sociological, economical, and cultural changes before and after the coup of 1898. Sponsored by the Cape Fear Museum.

November 5-7, 1998
Shall We Gather at the River?
This Christian Community Development Conference included models of reconciliation, meetings for pastors and business leaders, a prayer and healing walk through Wilmington, youth leadership development, economic initiatives, intercessory prayer for the city, practical workshops from national leaders, and a city-wide worship service. Sponsored by the Wilmington Leadership Foundation.

November 7, 1998
African-American Builders and Architects in North Carolina
A Bellamy Mansion Museum exhibit of physical remnants and artifacts

November 8, 1998
Service of Remembrance and Reconciliation
Led by Dr. Clifford A. Jones, Sr., past president of the NC General Baptist Convention and noted author and world renowned preacher. Co-sponsored by the Wilmington Interdenominational Ministerial Alliance and the 1898 Ministerial Roundtable.

November 10, 1998
1898 — An American Coup
A radio drama starring Rhonda Bellamy, Lloyd Wilson, Scott Simpson, George Scheibner, and Harvard Jennings, with appearances by National Public Radio's Carl Kasell and John Stempin. Written by Philip Gerard, author of *Cape Fear Rising*. Produced by Aileen LeBlanc. Sponsored by WHQR Public Radio.

*Rebroadcast Saturday, November 14

Commemorative Drama

"No More Sorrow to Arise"

An original play by Anne Russell

History repeated itself at Thalian Hall with the commemorative drama, *No More Sorrow to Arise* by Wilmington playwright Anne Russell. Told through actual letters Carrie Sadgwar Manly wrote her grown sons, Milo and Lewin, the original play recounted the tragic events of 1898 as written by the widow of black newspaperman Alex Manly.

An editorial by Alex Manly responding to an article by a white woman set off the political *coup d'etat* that resulted in the burning of the *Record*. Written in her Philadelphia home, Carrie Manly's personal missives tell the story of the family's exile from Wilmington.

"Carrie Manly's letters portray the times of slavery, of emancipation, of achievement, of oppression, of exile. They are filled with references to ordinary daily life and family interactions which transcend race. These comments personalize the events of 1898, so that it is no longer an anonymous historical event," wrote Russell.

The play's title is borrowed from one of the letters, which are maintained by the Bahai's of Wilmington

"I selected this passage because it evokes the spirituals which sustained the oppressed African-Americans, and it implies the healing which it is hoped will come from the 1898 commemoration. The word "arise" is dynamic, a call to aroused consciousness on the part of all of us who live now, one hundred years after the 1898 event," Russell continued.

More than one thousand people attended the 1998 production, which was staged at Thalian Hall, the site where the "White Man's Declaration of Independence" was first read and signed in 1898.

In addition to the Manlys, the drama included the characters of Col. Alfred Waddell, lawyers John and Marsden Bellamy, the Redshirts, the Secret Nine, a white pastor and a black pastor. Scenes took place at City Hall, Alexander Sprunt & Son wharf, and the First Ward in Wilmington's Brooklyn neighborhood.

"I am a licensed psychotherapist...and I know that healing cannot begin until an emotional or psychological wound is exposed and cleansed. Since a conspiracy of silence has long existed about the truth of 1898, the first step in healing has been to speak the truth aloud, to examine it and come to understand it. The serious repercussions of this event, the abiding residual anger resulting from this violation of human rights and of democratic principles, must be laid bare. Then, and only then, can reconstruction begin."

The production, staged November 5-7, 1998 on the mainstage of Thalian Hall, featured local actors Aisha Irving, Daren Beatty, and Antoinette Gazda and was directed by the late Margaret Freeman.

The drama was funded by the North Carolina Cultural Resources Commission, the North Carolina Arts Council, and the New York Times Foundation.

> *I came across Carrie Manly's letters and they touched me deeply. I knew that somehow her voice must be heard, for it is the voice of reason and determination and compassion, the voice of righteous indignation devoid of hatred.*
>
> Anne Russell
> Playwright

Antoinette Gazda (rear), Aisha Irving and Daren Beatty
in *No More Sorrow Arise*.
Courtesy of *Star News*

Cast of Characters

Antoinette Gazda	Real Carrie
Daren Beatty	Alex Manly
Aisha Irving	Dream Carrie
Sunday Muslim	Emmaline
John Henry Scott	Mick
Maxwell O. Paige	Rev. J.A. Kirk
Mick McGovern	Waddell
Shaun Mitchell	Henry
Todd Squires	Lawyer #1
Howard Asberry	Lawyer #2
Ray Bednarski	Rev. Trimble
T.J. Morris	Aristocrat #1
Robert Schaff	Aristocrat #2

Black Church Choir
Louise Harrison, Bertha Quince
Tamekia Bordeaux, Alfred Robertson
Thomas Sweet, Charles Davis (The Joyful Sounds)

White Church Choir
Amanda McCullough, Jude Cobley
Neal Dyson, John Taylor, Brian Workman, David Brown
Matthew TenHuisen, Kenny Bizzell, Dallas Midgett

Anne Russell has earned a Ph.D. in American Studies from the University of Hawaii, an MS in Urban Studies from Georgia State University, an MFA in Creative Writing from the University of North Carolina at Wilmington, and she is a certified mediator. She is currently on the faculty at the University of North Carolina at Wilmington and has also taught at St. Andrews College and Barton College. A former entertainment editor of the Raleigh *News and Observer*, she was also director of the arts for the City of Raleigh. Her writing includes *Wilmington, A Pictorial History*, the 1898 commemorative drama, *No More Sorrow to Arise*, *The Talented Tenth* documentary, and the screenplay *Midnight at the School for Common Sense* which depicts the life of the legendary Fort Fisher Hermit.

Partners for Economic Inclusion

By Si Cantwell, with Arlene Lawson

"If you say 'inclusion' in Jacksonville real fast, they say 'God bless you,' " a black businessman said to laughter at the 2004 annual meeting of Partners for Economic Inclusion. Thomas Patrick said his Jacksonville, N.C.-based consulting and training company did most of its business in Wilmington, thanks to contacts he made through the organization. "What you're doing sets the tone for North Carolina," he said.

In 1998, the 1898 Foundation set a goal of improving the economic prospects of black people. Toward that end, the Partners for Economic Inclusion formed to promote inclusion of black businesses and to find ways to level the playing field.

The founders were Rob Gerlach, president of The VTA Group, and Peter Grear, publisher of The Challenger newspaper. It was sponsored in early years by the N.C. Black Chamber of Commerce and the Greater Wilmington Chamber of Commerce, offering networking and educational opportunities and much more.

Tangible and Measurable Results

One initiative encouraged bankers to meet with black business owners. The "bank calling program" generated $1.6 million in loans in 2000, $2.8 million in 2001, $5.5 million in 2002 and more than $10 million in 2003. After that, bankers said the efforts continued but regulators frowned on tallying loans by racial categories.

Another initiative was the Economic Inclusion Model, which encouraged minority participation in construction of the New Hanover County jail, where the county gave around 20 percent of the contracts to small businesses and minority contractors.

Growing out of that effort, the Inclusion Coalition Board of large area employers in the public and private sectors was formed to try to steer business to minority-owned enterprises. It has held procurement summits for small and diverse businesses, creating opportunities for small and diverse businesses to obtain business from members.

In 2006, the Wilmington chapter of the N.C. Black Chamber of Commerce became the Black Chamber Council of the Greater Wilmington Chamber of Commerce.

Arlene Lawson, corporate community development officer of First Citizen Bank and Trust Company, and one of Partners' last set of co-leaders, said that after a decade of working to improve the prospects of black-owned businesses, the Partners for Economic Inclusion felt it was time in 2008 to pass the torch to organizations such as the Black Chamber Council.

2008 Partners Co-Chair Arlene Lawson recognizes founding Co-Chairs Rob Gerlach and Peter Greer at the sunset event.

Courtesy of *Star News*

Mission

To lead and facilitate dialogue and develop strategies for economic inclusiveness in the Lower Cape Fear Region which will create greatly expanded business opportunities for the African-American community.

As we identify obstacles that impede inclusive business practices, we will employ corrective actions that will establish the region as a competitive and ethnically diversified economy for the 21st century.

Founding Co-Chairs
Rob Gerlach and Peter Grear

Capital Team
Co-Leaders:
Wes Beckner and Gerry McCants

Define ways for black businesses to obtain capital for business start-up, expansion and working capital. Provide counseling and guidance to black-owned businesses to help them develop a business plan and connect their plan with capital resources. The goal was to improve knowledge of the process for obtaining capital and to identify sources of capital.

(Top and Right) Business leaders gather for the final Partners for Economic Inclusion Conference featuring Wilmington native, Phillip Clay, chancellor of the Massachusetts Institute of Technology.

Relationship Team
Co-Leaders:
Bill Holt and Linda Pearce

Create and implement ongoing processes for relationship building and networking among black and white business leaders. The team goal is to increase business opportunities and revenue for black businesses.

Education Team
Co-Leaders:
Peter Grear and Lesley Langer

Initiate methods for creating and implementing mentoring programs which will educate black entrepreneurs on how to operate and maintain a competitive business. The intended result is to increase the amount of practical business knowledge and experience of the black entrepreneur.

Sky Robinson

by Si Cantwell

Partners for Economic Inclusion was formed by the 1898 Foundation to improve the economic prospects of black people.

Marion "Sky" Robinson said he has benefited from that initiative.

Robinson operates Sky's Custom Welding, working at construction sites and machine shops. He established the company in the early 1990s.

He grew up in the Castle Hayne area. In 1965, he moved to Newport News, Va., and learned welding while working for Newport News Shipbuilding and Dry Dock Co.

He returned in 1972 and joined a local metalworking company. After it went out of business, he started Sky's Custom Welding in the 1990s. "When I first went into business," he said, "it seemed like there weren't many opportunities for blacks."

He began talking to Pat Melvin, then assistant New Hanover County manager. Melvin helped him make contacts.

"She started the ball rolling," he said.

And when Partners was formed in 1998, Melvin was there and so was Robinson.

Partners "really opened the doors in the areas of networking and also education," Robinson said. "Partners also made me look at my business and look at where I needed to be stronger."

Programs at Cape Fear Community College and the University of North Carolina Wilmington taught him how to read blueprints and how to compete for contracts.

"And the banks were excellent," he said. "We got to know the bankers personally."

"Today, black contractors are able to do more than we were 13 years ago," he said. "Everybody knows someone now, and Partners had a lot to do with that."

photo by John W. Davis

Partners for Economic Inclusion

2008 Leadership Team

Harold Beatty
Jerome Belton
Patrick Boykin
Bruce Cavenaugh
Laura Ess
Rob Gerlach
Peter Grear
Vance Green
Robert Gruber
Randall Johnson
Jonathan Krieps
Leslie Langer
Arlene Lawson, Chair
Pat Melvin
Howard Rasheed
Nick Rhodes
Anita Roberts
Boyd Robison
Louis H. Rogers III
Cheryl Sutton

Ex Officio Members

Tim Brewington
Dennis Carter
Larry Clark
Al Corbett
Windell Daniels (late)
Todd Gerlach
Herbert Harris
Henry Hebel
Paul Hicks
Matt Magne
Connie Majure-Rhett
Phil Marion
Gerry McCants
Hank Miller
Laura W. Padgett
Linda Pearce
Linda Upperman Smith
Beth White Steelman
Clyde Stunson
Bob Warwick
Ken Weeden
Resea Willis

Ministerial Roundtable

Statement of Purpose

The Ministerial Roundtable is a group of ministers in the greater Wilmington area, which is committed to resisting racism in our own lives, in our congregations, and in our community. The Roundtable was organized in 1998 by the 1898 Centennial Foundation to bring clergy together to participate in the commemoration of the 1898 *coup d'etat* in Wilmington.

The Ministerial Roundtable is committed to gathering together in order to forge friendships with one another, to seek a clearer understanding of God's will for human community, to encourage one another to engage our congregations in the struggle against racism, and to be faithful participants in the racial healing we believe God is carrying out in our nation.

We believe God calls us to repent of attitudes which demean others, to repent of institutional practices which foster homogeneous worship and religious life, and to repent of and correct injustices in our city and nation which deny life as God intended it for all people.

We believe that peace eludes all members of a society wherever any are hated or oppressed.

We believe that a change in society toward greater acceptance of people of all races will not happen unless racist patterns of thought and interactions are intentionally challenged and replaced with words and actions which reflect the vision God has placed before us of a loving, just and tolerant world.

We invite ministers of all faiths to join with us in this endeavor.

Ministerial Roundtable of Wilmington
1999-2008

The Rev. Roland Banks, Windemere Presbyterian
* The Rev. Mary & Elder Lenzey Benjamin, Undenominational Pentecostal
The Rev. Shawn Blackwelder, Fifth Avenue United Methodist
The Rev. Blair Both, Church of the Servant Episcopal
The Rev. Bill Braswell, Pine Valley United Methodist
The Rev. Joseph Brown, St. Luke AME Zion, Co-Chair 2002, 2005
Carl A Byrd, Sr., Director, New Hanover Human Relations Commission
* The Rev. Johnny Calhoun, St. Stephen AME, Co-Chair 2000, 2001
The Rev. Robert Campbell, New Beginnings Community Church
The Rev. Lily Chou, Fifth Avenue United Methodist
Pastor Paul E. Christ, Kure Memorial Lutheran
* The Rev. Joseph Cooper, Church of the Servant Episcopal
The Rev. Allen Cottemond, Shiloh Missionary Baptist
The Rev. Bill Cottingham, Trinity United Methodist
The Rev. Richard G. Elliott, St. Andrew's On-The-Sound Episcopal
The Rev. D.K. Ferguson, Shiloh Missionary Baptist, Co-Chair 2006-2008
The Rev. Keith Gregg, Carolina Beach Presbyterian
The Rev. Perry Griffin, Chestnut St. Presbyterian
The Rev. Raleigh Hairston, St. Mark's Episcopal
The Rev. Russell D. Heiland, Jr., Unity Christ Church
* The Rev. June Highfill, Pearsall Memorial Presbyterian, Co-Chair 2000-2005
The Rev. Matt Highfill, Winter Park Presbyterian
The Rev. Rick Houston, Pilgrim Rest Missionary Baptist
* The Rev. Lone Jensen, Unitarian-Universalist Fellowship
The Rev. Susan Karlson, Unitarian-Universalist Fellowship, Co-Chair 2006-2008
The Rev. Robert Kus, St. Mary's Catholic
The Rev. Amanda McCullough, St. Jude's Metropolitan Community Church
The Rev. David McDonald, Westminster Presbyterian
The Rev. James Malloy, Fifth Avenue United Methodist
The Rev. Bob Millis, Ogden Baptist
The Rev. Aaron Moore, AMEZ
The Rev. Bob Morrison, St. John's Episcopal
The Rev. Rene Pare, United Christ Church
* The Rev. H.H. Parker, AME
The Rev. Kathy Reinger, First Christian
The Rev. Maurice Ritchie, United Methodist
Imam Abdul Shareef, Tauheed Islamic Center
The Rev. Sam Murrell, UNCW
Rabbi Ben Romer, Temple of Israel
The Rev. Adrian Shepard, United Advent Christian
The Rev. Don Skinner, Phoenix Employment Services of Wilmington, Inc.
The Rev. Linda Taylor, Oleander United Methodist and Devon Park United Methodist
The Rev. Steve Teague, St. James Episcopal
* The Rev. James Utley, The Love Center Church, Co-Chair 2003-2004
The Rev. Maxine Utley, The Love Center Church
The Rev. Hannah Vaughan, Presbyterian Church U.S.A.
The Rev. Dan Warnes, Church of the Reconciliation Lutheran
* Rabbi Robert Waxman, B'nai Israel Synagogue
The Rev. Dan Webster, First Christian

* Founding members

Barbara Sullivan and Michael Murchison

Barbara Sullivan grew up in Princeton, New Jersey, graduating from Miss Fine's School in 1966. She received her B.A. from Middlebury College in 1971 and her J.D. from George Washington University Law School in 1975. After working as a Foreign Service Officer for the U.S. State Department and as a civil rights lawyer for the U.S. Department of Labor, she moved to Wilmington in 1983 with her husband, Michael, and their daughter, Rachel. Their son,

Barbara has served as board member and president of WHQR public radio, Chamber Music Wilmington and the 1898 Foundation. She has also served on the boards of Parents Community Preschool, New Horizons Elementary School, and the YWCA. She worked on the 1898 Memorial Park Committee from 2000-2008.

Michael Murchison, a native of Wilmington, graduated from New Hanover High School in 1967. He went on to receive a B.A. from Amherst College in 1971 and a J.D. degree from Cornell Law School in 1974. After working with the National Labor Relations Board and the U.S. Environmental Protection Agency in Washington, DC, he moved back to Wilmington in 1983 to join the law firm founded by his father, Wallace Murchison. At the firm, Murchison Taylor attorneys, he specializes in labor and employment law, health law and general litigation. In 2007 he received the Addison Hewlett, Jr. Award for his *pro bono* legal work.

Michael has served as a board member and president of the Coastal Land Trust, the Historic Wilmington Foundation and the Wilmington Tree Commission, and as a board member of the Brooklyn Arts Center, Cameron Art Museum, and the Wilmington Concert Association. He enjoys playing on several USTA tennis teams in the Wilmington area.

Charles, was born in Wilmington in 1985. Barbara worked part-time as a French teacher, a mediator and on the staff of a Latino outreach center in Wilmington. She is the author of *Garden Perennials for the Coastal South*, published by the University of North Carolina at Chapel Hill. She is a lecturer, magazine writer and radio commentator on the topic of gardening.

Peace Circle

William Dean Bryant

A native of Pender County, North Carolina, William Dean Bryant received his bachelor's degree from Lincoln University in Pennsylvania and master's degree from the University of Pennsylvania at Philadelphia. Further graduate studies were undertaken at North Carolina A&T University, North Carolina Central University, East Carolina University, North Carolina State University, the University of Dayton, Rutgers University, Ohio State University, and the University of North Carolina at Chapel Hill.

Bryant was director of Occupational Education for Greensboro City Schools. From 1966 to 1973, Bryant worked in the Executive and Professional Placement Office of the National Cash Register Company, with headquarters in Dayton, Ohio. He previously taught in the Occupational Education field in Duplin and New Hanover County Schools. He also taught extension courses in Wilmington and Raleigh for North Carolina State University, University of North Carolina at Wilmington, Cape Fear Technical Institute, and North Carolina A&T University.

Bryant was a veteran of World War II with service in France, Germany, England, Italy, Belgium, Turkey, Iran, Iraq, Jerusalem, Australia, New Zealand, India, the Hawaiian Islands, and Africa.

He was a former Basileus of Omicron Alpha Chapter of Omega Psi Phi Fraternity and also served on the boards of directors of United Way (Fund) of New Hanover County and the Wilmington Chapter of the American Red Cross. He was also a member of Optimist International and Phi Delta Kappa.

Bryant was a former president of the New Hanover Unit of the North Carolina Teachers Association, the Old North State Vocational Association, and the North Carolina Trade and Industrial Education Teachers Association, of which he was the first black to be elected as vice-president of the newly integrated group. He was chairman of the Talent Hunt Committee of the American Youth Industrial Education Association, a former coordinator for New Hanover County Schools, former chair of the North Carolina Students Industrial Organization

Talent Committee, which he organized and chaired for a period of more than 10 years, a former president of the Men's Council and an Elder at Chestnut Street Presbyterian Church.

He was appointed by former Governor Dan Moore to serve on the advisory committee of the North Carolina Good Neighbor Council and reappointed by Governor Scott. He was also appointed by the late Wilmington Mayor O.O. Allsbrook to serve on the Wilmington Good Neighbor Council. Governor Jim Hunt appointed him to the State Advisory Council on Vocational Education in 1977.

Other appointments included the State Advisory Committee to Trade and Industrial Education by Dr. A. Craig Phillips, state superintendent of public instruction and the Community College Instruction Commission by Dr. W. Dallas Herring, chair of the State Board of Education.

Bryant has received commendations from numerous institutions and influential Americans for his outstanding service, including Vice President Hubert Humphrey, Governor Jim Hunt, and Dr. L.H. Foster, president of Tuskegee Institute.

He is survived by his wife, Thelma Brewington Bryant, daughter Tanya Bryant Charles (Joseph), and granddaughter, Tawana Isaac.

Peace Circle

Bertha Boykin Todd & Family

Edward Mack Todd (deceased) was a native of Zebulon, North Carolina, the son of a Baptist minister. He spent his public school years in Raleigh and Smithfield and entered the military while attending Winston Salem State University. From 1943– 1946, Edward served in the United States Army with the European Theatre of Operation. He attained the rank of Master Sergeant.

Edward entered Shaw University upon returning from the military, where he earned a B.S. degree in health and physical education. He was later awarded a Master's Degree in health and physical education from North Carolina Central University in Durham. Post graduate degree studies were pursued at East Carolina University in Greenville.

Edward served in the New Hanover Public School System for 34 years. During this period, he served as a teacher of health and physical education, a coach, and an assistant principal. For many years, Edward served Chestnut Street Presbyterian Church (USA) as the Youth Sunday School teacher and as an Elder. He was also a member of Omega Psi Phi Fraternity. Mack was married to Bertha Boykin Todd for 42 years.

Bertha Boykin Todd, an identical twin, was born in Sampson County where she received her public education prior to attending what is now known as North Carolina Central University. Her twin, Myrtle Sampson (Robert) is a retired university professor emeritus from NC A&T University. Bertha graduated with honors having majored in science. She continued her schooling at NCCU and earned a Master's Degree in Library Science. She then became an employee of the New Hanover County School System at Williston Senior High School in 1952. Several years later when Bertha was serving in administration at John T. Hoggard High School, she attended East Carolina University and earned two additional degrees: Master of Arts in Administration & Supervision and an Ed.S. in Administration and Supervision.

During the sixties, Bertha became intensely involved in civic work due to school desegregation. She served on local, state, and national levels in various capacities. Bertha had the opportunity to serve in several challenging positions while employed by the New Hanover County School system, including conducting the first county-wide book fair, serving as the first female secondary summer school principal, and serving as a storyteller for the New Hanover County Educational Television System.

Bertha retired from the school system after 39 years of service. Following retirement, Bertha served on numerous boards and as a motivational speaker. She served as the chairperson of the New Hanover County Human Relations Commission. She also served for eight years on the North Carolina Human Relations Council at the pleasure of Governor James B. Hunt. She also gave of her time serving as president of several civic organizations. Bertha is a former co-chair of the 1898 Centennial Foundation (i.e. The 1898 Foundation).

Bertha is a member of Chestnut Street Presbyterian Church (USA) where she has served as an elder, Sunday school teacher, moderator of several organizations, and a choir member. She has received many awards and honors, including the National Founders' Service Award from Alpha Kappa Alpha Sorority, Inc., Order of the Long Leaf Pine, the New Hanover County NAACP Award, an honorary Doctorate of Humanities degree from UNCW, YMCA Distinguished Educator Award, the Razor Walker Award (UNCW), The Wilmington Civitian Good Citizenship Award, The *Star News* Lifetime Achievement Award, the Paul Harris Fellow Award from Rotary International, and the Ladies of Legacy Award from Union Baptist Church. Bertha's coined motto is, "The pursuit of goals gives meaning to life." She and her late husband had two children, Rita Denise and Brian Edward. She also has several socially adopted sons and daughters.

Rita Denise Todd Griffin was born in Wilmington. After graduating from New Hanover High School in 1975, she matriculated to the University of North Carolina at Chapel Hill and earned a B.A. degree in Elementary Education. In December of 1993, she earned a Master of Arts degree in Elementary Education from the University of North Carolina at Wilmington. She subsequently earned a Principal's Certificate in 1995. Over the span of 28 years, Rita has taught in four counties in the state of North Carolina.

Rita is a member of Chestnut Street Presbyterian Church where she has served as a deacon, an elder and a member of two choirs. She currently performs duties as The Ivy Leaf Reporter as a member of the Alpha Psi Omega Chapter of Alpha Kappa Alpha Sorority, Inc. Rita is also a member of The Wilmington Chapter of The Links, Inc. and is married to the Reverend Perry Dwayne Griffin.

Perry Dwayne Griffin was born in Greenville, South Carolina and attended the public school system in Greenville. Following graduation from Woodmont High School, he attended Benedict College and Johnson C. Smith University. After receiving a Bachelor of Arts degree in sociology, Perry enrolled in the Interdenominational Theological Center at Johnson C. Smith University Seminary in Atlanta, Georgia. There he received his Master of Divinity degree in New Testament Biblical Studies and completed the denominational requirements for ordination. Rev. Griffin was ordained as a Minister of the Word and Sacrament in October of 1996. He has served as pastor of Chestnut Street Presbyterian Church in Wilmington since February of 1999. Perry is also a member of Phi Beta Sigma and has two sons, Peris Michael and Ian Marshall. His brother-in-law is Brian Edward Todd.

Brian Edward Todd was born in Wilmington. He graduated from New Hanover High School in 1979. Following high school graduation, Brian attended Embry Riddle Aeronautical University in Daytona Beach, Florida. There he earned a Bachelor of Science Degree in Aeronautical Science. Brian became a flight instructor at Aeronautical, Incorporated (Wilmington, NC). He also made several flights for Eastern Delivery also located in Wilmington. Subsequently, Brian performed duties as a pilot for American Eagle based in Lynchburg, Virginia before being employed by Delta Airlines in November of 1985. Currently, Brian is a captain with Delta and flies solely international trips.

During Brian's teen years, he served as President of the Wilmington Chapter of Jack & Jill of America, Inc. and sang in the youth choir at Chestnut Street Presbyterian Church (USA). For several years, Brian worked at a grocery store and delivered newspapers. He currently resides in Decatur, GA.

Todds and Sampsons

Rita Todd Griffin

Perry Griffin

Brian Todd

Peace Circle

Charlie West and Beverly Cree

Charlie West came to Wilmington in 1980 to teach business management in the Cameron School at the University of North Carolina at Wilmington. He retired as Associate Professor Emeritus in 1992. He had an earlier career as a professional manager with large corporations following his graduation from Cornell University with a B.E.E. in 1953 and M.B.A. in 1956. He spent two years in the U.S. Army Signal Corps, including a year in Korea. Before starting his teaching career, he received a Ph.D. in organizational behavior from the University of Louisville.

During his time in Wilmington, Charlie has had a special interest in the cause of racial justice. He was treasurer of the 1898 Foundation, member of the New Hanover County Human Relations Commission, and on the local governing boards of the NAACP and Girls, Inc. He was also an active member of the district antiracism committee of his church, the Unitarian Universalist Fellowship of Wilmington. He enjoyed his role in the Democratic Party, feeling this was an organization where people of color were fully empowered.

Beverly Cree and Charlie were married in 1992. Her career, as an early childhood specialist, focuses on working in a variety of ways with young children, their teachers, and their families. Recently she taught in the School of Education at the University of North Carolina at Wilmington. Her education includes a B.S. and M.S. in psychology, M.Ed. in education from the University of North Carolina at Wilmington, and a Ph.D. in child development from the University of North Carolina at Greensboro. She has been active on the boards of Domestic Violence Shelter & Services, the Carolina Vocal Arts Ensemble, and the Mountain Retreat & Conference Center, which has a focus on promoting peace in diverse relationships.

Peace Circle

The Family of Dr. Leroy W. Upperman

Leroy W. Upperman, M.D., born January 1, 1913, in Jersey City, New Jersey, son of a Pullman porter and boarding house owner, earned his B.S. from Lincoln University in 1934, and his M.D. from Howard University in 1938. He interned at Lincoln Hospital in Durham for one year, then became House Physician of Community Hospital in Wilmington from 1939 to 1941. He opened a private general medicine and surgical practice in Wilmington on North Seventh Street until he retired in 1991. He was active in the community, serving on various boards including the Community Boys and Girls Club, the United Fund, the Greater Wilmington Chamber of Commerce and the Human Relations Commission. He was a member of Chestnut Street Presbyterian Church, the Old North State Medical Society, the National Medical Association and was a lifetime member of the NAACP. He was a founding member of the Wilmington Chapter of Kappa Alpha Psi Fraternity. The University of North Carolina Wilmington dedicated its African-American Cultural Center to Dr. Upperman in 1996 after his death, in recognition of a trust he established that awarded over $400,000 to UNCW to fund multiple scholarships for African-American students and support programming at the center. He died February 20, 1996.

Callie Smith Upperman was born in Columbus County on February 11, 1924, daughter of a farmer and homemaker. She graduated from Lincoln Hospital School of Nursing in 1944 and moved to Wilmington to work as a public health nurse. She met her future husband while in Wilmington. They married in 1947. Two children were born to them, Leroy W. Upperman, Jr. and Linda Carol Upperman. Callie was very active in the community and a strong advocate for educational equality as the schools were segregated at that time. She was a member of the Wilmington Chapter of Links, Inc., Jack and Jill, and Chestnut Street Presbyterian Church. She died September 19, 1973.

Leroy W. Upperman, Jr., born March 22, 1948, received his undergraduate and law degrees from the University of North Carolina at Chapel Hill in 1970 and 1973. He was admitted to the North Carolina Bar in 1973. He maintained a general law practice in Greensboro, NC, until he relocated to Los Angeles, CA, in the late 1970s where he pursued a career in commercial real estate until his death in 1991.

Linda Upperman Smith, born May 31, 1949, earned her B.S. in French from Spelman College in 1972, a M.L.S. from the University of Southern California in 1976, and a M.S.W. from U.C.L.A. in 1982. She was awarded her L.C.S.W. in 1985 and maintained a private clinical practice in the Los Angeles area until 1996. She returned to the Wilmington area in 1997. She has served on the UNCW Board of Trustees, UNCW Foundation Board, Wachovia Bank Advisory Board, 1898 Foundation, Partners for Economic Inclusion Board and the Thalian Hall Center for the Performing Arts. Her passion was diversity scholarship fundraising at UNCW. Two sons were born to her: Robert Lewis Ross, Jr., August 22, 1970, and Christopher Michael Chang-Ross, September 28, 1972. Her sons and daughter-in-law, Aurora Chang-Ross, earned undergraduate degrees at the University of California Berkeley. In 2005 Linda married Howard S. Rasheed, Ph.D., a business professor at the University of North Carolina Wilmington.

Peace Circle

In Memory of

Samuel Joseph Howie, Jr.
1921-1988

Samuel Joseph Howie, Jr. graduated from Williston Industrial High School. He received the B.S. degree in mathematics and science from Livingstone College and the M.S. degree in school administration and supervision from Cornell University. Further studies were undertaken at Cornell University, North Carolina Central University and East Carolina University.

He held positions in the education profession as teacher, department chairman, assistant principal, principal, director, assistant superintendent, and certified consultant to the North Carolina Secondary Committee for the Southern Association of Colleges and Schools.

He retired from the New Hanover County school system on July 31, 1986 after 44 years of service.

Mr. Howie was affiliated with numerous educational and community organizations and agencies. Among these he was a member of the board of directors of the Community Boys Club, Family Services, Cape Fear Area United Way, New Hanover County Retired School Personnel Association, National Association of Secondary School Principals, North Carolina Association of Administrators, Phi Delta Kappa educational fraternity, and chairman of the trustee board of St. Luke A.M.E. Zion Church. He also served as Director of Christian Education, Cape Fear Conference, from 1947-1977, and was a choir member for many years.

Mr. Howie is listed in *Who's Who in American Education*. He received state and national recognition from the North Carolina State Education Agency and the U.S. Office of Education for implementing an exemplary Compensatory Education program in reading and mathematics in the New Hanover County Schools system. He was named New Hanover County Administrator of the Year for 1982-83.

He was married to Lydia Staton Howie, a retired school administrator. He has two sons: Samuel J. Howie, III, a guidance counselor at Murray Middle School in New Hanover County; and Herschel Wayne Howie, promotions/marketing producer for WECT-TV in Wilmington.

He died February 20, 1988.

Memorials

The S.J. Howie, Jr. Award for Leadership and Service was established in 1988 by the Cape Fear chapter of Phi Delta Kappa and is given annually in recognition of outstanding service and leadership in education.

The Department of Christian Education at St. Luke A.M.E. Zion Church established the S.J. Howie, Jr. Scholarship in 1999. It is awarded to graduating seniors who actively participate in programs sponsored by the A.M.E. Zion Church on the local, district, and conference levels.

Peace Circle

Historic Wilmington Foundation, Inc.

"To protect and preserve the irreplaceable historic resources of Wilmington and the Lower Cape Fear region."

Since 1966, the Historic Wilmington Foundation has worked to protect the irreplaceable architectural and historical resources of Wilmington and the Lower Cape Fear region. The Foundation was organized by a group of citizens concerned by the demolition of Wilmington's historic resources and the deterioration of its downtown.

With the HWF's innovative revolving loan – the first of its kind in North Carolina – the organization was able to buy historic properties and place them under the protection of preservation covenants before selling them for rehabilitation. Almost 100 properties have been directly saved by the HWF, and hundreds more have been preserved due to the foundation's influence. When all other options were exhausted, Historic Wilmington Foundation has also saved houses by having them moved and rehabilitated on a new lot.

The Foundation's unique plaque program recognizes the historical significance of commercial buildings, homes and cemeteries over 75 years old (50 years in beach communities). Over 475 plaques have been researched and approved for historic buildings throughout New Hanover County and beyond. The research is kept on file at HWF headquarters, as well as in the North Carolina Room of the New Hanover County Library.

The HWF's educational offerings include seminars, exhibits and lectures on topics such as the Lost Buildings of Wilmington. A popular, intensive workshop on the rehabilitation of historic buildings, Preservation for Profit, features expert advice concerning preservation tax credits, historic districts, building code and financing. Each year, the organization hosts tours of historic churches, neighborhoods, and cemeteries, often focusing on the works of a particular builder or designer.

To celebrate National Preservation Month, Historic Wilmington holds events throughout the month of May. Beginning in 2006, the organization began announcing its annual list of Most Threatened Historic Places of the Lower Cape Fear region during Preservation Month. By drawing attention to endangered properties, this new initiative has already made a significant impact: three sites have been saved. The month's festivities are capped by the presentation of the Preservation Awards, which honor local projects and achievements in restoration, infill construction, rehabilitation, as well as personal contributions to the preservation field.

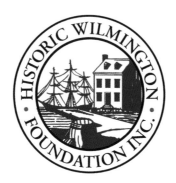

During April's Azalea Festival, the Foundation presents the popular Wilmington House Tour, featuring historic and contemporary houses of various styles. The organization recently renewed the popular 5K Run for Preservation, a unique midweek evening race through historic downtown Wilmington held in the fall.

HWF is an invaluable resource for our community, offering advice and technical assistance on historical renovations, preservation tax credits, and preservation zoning questions. Historic Wilmington also advocates with all local government for good planning and development as well as the protection of historic resources. The Foundation has played an integral role in the establishment of all of Wilmington's National Register Districts, as well as our local historic districts.

The Historic Wilmington Foundation is a non-profit membership organization. The organization receives no federal or state funding, relying solely on the generosity of its members and supporters to accomplish its mission. Funding sources include membership dues, corporate and private gifts, foundation grants and money collected via fundraising events.

516 North Fourth Street,
Wilmington, NC 28401
Telephone: 910.762.2511
Fax: 910.762.1551
www.historicwilmington.org

Peace Circle

In Memory of

Alice Borden Moore Sisson

1918-2004

"The legacy of role models like Alice Sisson endures…. Alice, whose memory is indelibly etched in this community, will always stand for self-sacrifice, grace, strength, and compassion."

Sid Bradsher, retired exec. director of Family Services
Melissa Bass, former student intern and family therapist

Alice Borden Moore Sisson was born in Wilmington, October 10, 1918, the daughter of the late Roger and Alice Wallace Moore. She was a faithful member of St. Andrews Covenant Presbyterian Church for 74 years, where she served as an Elder and Sunday School teacher.

She received her master's degree in social work from the University of North Carolina at Chapel Hill in 1972 and served as an inspiring family therapist and clinical social worker with Family Services of the Lower Cape Fear for 32 years.

Alice's loving contributions to the well-being of the community are legend. She served as president of the Wilmington chapter of the Junior League and was a founding member of Food Bank of the Lower Cape Fear, Southeastern Mental Health Center, Family Services of the Lower Cape Fear, New Hanover Sheltered Workshop, YWCA's Legal Access for Women, and the Domestic Violence Task Force.

She received wide recognition for her many contributions: honorary member of Wilmington Rotary Club, North Carolina Social Worker of the Year Award (1989), honoree of Elderhaus (2001), and the YWCA's Woman of Achievement Award.

She died July 31, 2004 after a brief illness.

She is survived by her son, William Sisson, Jr. (Joy Miller), daughters Penny Rushmore (Dean), and Fran Gibson, and seven grandchildren.

She was preceded in death by her husband, William E. Sisson, Sr., and her brothers, Roger Moore, Jr. and Edwin Moore.

Founders Circle

Worldwide Reach, World Renowned Quality, Firmly rooted in Wilmington for more than 22 years

PPD is a leading global contract research organization providing drug discovery, development and post-approval services as well as compound partnering programs. From its worldwide headquarters in Wilmington, PPD's reach spans six continents with offices in 31 countries and more than 10,400 professionals. Our employees work with pride and unwavering integrity to help our clients and partners accelerate delivery of safe and effective therapeutics to patients.

We strive for excellence in all we do, both in being a global leader in our industry and in embracing the responsibilities of corporate citizenship in the communities where we do business.

We are dedicated to practicing global diversity and believe it is our responsibility to help strengthen the communities in which we live and work.

We encourage employee involvement and volunteerism and believe that our participation is more than just good corporate citizenship – it's a matter of investing in each other.

No one gets medicine into the system faster®

Worldwide Headquarters | 929 North Front Street | Wilmington, N.C. 28401-3331 | +1 910 251 0081
www.ppdi.com

Peace Circle

In Memoriam

Sarah Lee White

1923-2004

Sarah Lee White was born in Sampson County to the late Milford Lee and Mary E. Lee. She graduated from Clinton High School, furthering her education at Fayetteville State University and at North Carolina A & T University, where she earned a Master's Degree. Continued studies, which led to certification as a Speech-Language Clinician, were completed at North Carolina Central University, East Carolina University, and the University of North Carolina at Wilmington. She served the New Hanover County School System as a teacher and speech clinician for more than 30 years.

Her professional and social affiliations included: Retired Teachers of the Cape Fear Area, Retired School Personnel of New Hanover County, Fayetteville State University Alumni Association, Daughters of Isis, Alpha Kappa Alpha Sorority and Jack and Jill of America, Inc.

Mrs. White was an active communicant of St. Mark's Episcopal Church, where she served as the Senior Warden, President of the Episcopal Church Woman and Sunday School teacher. She was also a member of St. Anne's Guild, the St. Mary's Altar Guild, and St. Cecelia's Choir.

She was married to the late educator Kenneth C. White and was also preceded in death by her daughter, Etta White Davis. She is survived by a grandson, Kenneth Cornelius Davis.

The late Kenneth White was born in Baltimore, Maryland, but moved to Wilmington at an early age. He attended the public schools of New Hanover County and was a member of the Williston Industrial High School Class of 1945. White attended Fayetteville State University on an athletic scholarship and graduated with a B.S. in Education. He later received an M.S. degree from North Carolina A & T University and completed requirements for the principal's certificate. Further studies included credits at East Carolina and the University of North Carolina at Wilmington.

His 36-year career as an educator included two years each at Roseboro High School in Sampson County and Bladen County Training School in Elizabethtown. He spent 32 years in New Hanover County Public Schools, including positions as assistant principal at D.C. Virgo School and as principal at John J. Blair and Williston Junior High School. He was principal at J.C. Roe Elementary School at the time of his death on March 22, 1986.

His professional affiliations included the New Hanover County Principals' Association, North Carolina Association of Educators, North Carolina Council of International Reading Association, North Carolina Association of School Administrators, and the North Carolina Athletic Officials Association.

Fraternal affiliations included Habib Shrine Temple #159, Hanover Lodge #14, Consistory #63, Les Gents, Community Boys Club, Port City Golfers Association, and the Coastal Athletic Association, of which he served as president.

Being very active in religious activities, he served on numerous boards and committees at St. Mark's Episcopal Church.

Founders Circle

In Memoriam
Luther Jordan
1950-2002

The late Luther Henry Jordan, Jr. was first elected to the North Carolina Senate District 7 seat in 1993, representing New Hanover, Pender, Brunswick, Lenoir, Onslow and Jones counties. During his five terms in office, he served

in numerous capacities including Majority Whip, Minority Whip, chairman of the Justice and Public Safety Committee, vice chairman of the State and Local Government Committee, second vice-chairman of the North Carolina Democratic Party, and chairman of the North Carolina Legislative Black Caucus.

Prior to serving in the North Carolina Senate, Luther Jordan served on Wilmington City Council for 16 years and was the first black Mayor Pro-Tempore for the City of Wilmington.

A 1969 graduate of New Hanover High School, Jordan earned an associate's degree in Funeral Services from Gupton Jones College of Mortuary Science in 1972, and a bachelor of arts degree in Liberal Studies from Shaw University in 1997.

Luther Jordan, Jr. was owner and president of Jordan Funeral Home, established in 1944 by his parents, the late Daisy Fields Jordan and Luther Henry Jordan, Sr. The modest family business was operated by Daisy Jordan and William

Chestnut after the demise of Luther Jordan, Sr. in 1969. After completing a degree in mortuary science and receiving his funeral service license, Luther Jordan, Jr. began assisting in the funeral home's operation. In 1978, the business was incorporated as Jordan Funeral Home, Inc., with Daisy Jordan as president and treasurer, while Luther Jr. served as vice-president. Due to the declining health of Daisy Jordan, she designated her son to operate the family business in 1987. The Jordan Funeral Home-Columbus County Chapel was also established that year. Other dedicated staff members included secretary Carolyn Logan and manager William O. Boykin.

In 1998, construction began on a new funeral home at South Fifth Avenue and Dawson Street. Due to Luther Jordan's health, his daughter Kisha Renee Jordan obtained her funeral directing license and continued to work in the family business. During that time she pursued a Bachelor of Arts degree in Business Management with a concentration in Public Administration and a Master of Arts degree in Human Resources.

Senator Jordan was very involved in the community, serving on the boards of directors of Wachovia Bank and Shaw University. He was a member of the Omicron Alpha Chapter of Omega Psi Phi Fraternity, Hanover Lodge #14 F & AM (PHA), Wilmington Consistory #63, Habib Temple #159, the Wilmington Sportsman Club, East Coast Trail Riders, and Past Exalted Ruler Leading Lodge I.B.P.O.E.W. He was a member of Chestnut Street Presbyterian Church, where he served as an elder, deacon, trustee and member of the Men's Council.

Luther Jordan, Jr. was a loving father, caring friend, great politician, mortician and businessman. He is survived by three daughters, Kisha Renee Jordan, Angela Rhodes, and Tamela Malloy, all of Wilmington.

Peace Circle

In Memoriam

Ernest Adison Swain

A native of Southport, North Carolina, Ernest A Swain graduated from Brunswick County Training School in 1933. Upon graduation he attended Morehouse College in Atlanta, graduating with an ABA degree in General Education and History in 1938. He returned to his hometown to begin a career in teaching in Brunswick County Schools. His teaching career was cut short when he was drafted into the United States Army, completing a 26-month tour of duty for which he received an honorable discharge.

Returning to southeastern North Carolina, he was offered a position as a Probation/Truant Officer with New Hanover County. He served in that capacity for two years, until C.S. McDonald, principal of Peabody and Dudley elementary schools offered him the position of Assistant Principal and Coach. To become more effective in his role as an educator, Ernest Swain enrolled at Chicago University during the summer months, receiving a Master of Arts degree from the Division of Social Science in 1953.

His lifelong career as an educator included serving as principal of James B. Dudley, Peabody, and William H. Hooper elementary schools. He served on numerous boards in the City of Wilmington and New Hanover County, including serving as vice chairman of the New Hanover County Board of Elections. He saw this role as ironic given that he was once a victim of voter registration discrimination in the 1930s when he was initially denied the right to register and vote in Brunswick County.

A member of St. Luke African Methodist Episcopal Zion Church in Wilmington, he was also a member of Omicron Alpha Chapter of Omega Psi Phi Fraternity for more than 50 years.

A merit scholarship has been established on his behalf at the University of North Carolina Wilmington. The Ernest A Swain Merit Scholarship, established by the Omicron Alpha Chapter of Omega Psi Phi Fraternity, aims to attract freshmen from underserved popula-

tions. Recipients must be graduates of the New Hanover, Brunswick, or Pender County school systems. Eligible students must demonstrate academic ability and the superior qualities and characteristics embodied by Mr. Swain through his decades of selfless leadership in the African-American community. In addition, recipients must demonstrate leadership through volunteer community service in the communities where they live.

Peace Circle

James Brown, M.D. and Family

James Brown was born in New York City to Louise Brown and David Brown just after the 1929 stock market crash. One of five siblings (David Anthony Brown, Dorothy Brown Gray, Lizzie Brown Hampton and Erma McCoy Chambers), he did not live in New York long enough to claim the city as his home, as his mother Louise chose to return to her hometown of Wilmington, North Carolina.

Louise, the daughter of Thalia Howe Whitfield and the great-granddaughter of noted Wilmington builder Alfred Howe, preferred to be closer to her mother and to raise her children in the south as opposed to the hustle and bustle of New York City. However, life was not easy during the days following the stock market crash. Nonetheless, she was able to earn a living, and settled into the Brooklyn community in Wilmington. David Brown remained in New York City and died some years later. Louise ultimately remarried to Rufus McCoy of Duplin County and relocated to Pennsylvania where Rufus made a living in the steel industry while she pursued a career in nursing. Although Rufus is now deceased, at the time of this printing she continues to live in Pennsylvania.

Growing up in Wilmington was not easy for James and his siblings for he came to understand poverty and its effects on a family. As young boys, he and his brother Anthony worked to help their mother by performing various chores and tasks at home and for neighbors. As a reward, he received opportunities to visit the home of the Parsley family on Masonboro Sound where his grandmother Thalia was the family cook. There he would catch fish and crabs on the sound and enjoy special treats prepared by his grandmother. It was during those times that his grandmother would share stories of the 1898 racial massacre in Wilmington and her eyewitness accounts of the chaos on the streets of Brooklyn on the morning of November 14, 1898. She shared stories of how her father, William C. Howe and other men were unable to obtain ammunition for hunting from local merchants weeks before the event. Although he worked in steady employment on the waterfront in Wilmington, he, as other men of African descent, relied on hunting in the local forests to supplement the family meals. In addition, she recalled her experiences of hiding with her family and many other women and children in the wooded burial grounds just east of Brooklyn, and now known as Pine Forest Cemetery.

It was these stories and the strong values on which he was raised that instilled in him a deep appreciation for understanding one's heritage, educating oneself and your children and achieving a degree of socio-economic success to ensure the stability and growth of one's family tree. Without strong families, Dr. Brown believes we cannot have strong communities and ultimately a strong country.

Educated in the public schools of Wilmington, James attended Peabody Elementary School and ultimately graduated from Williston Senior High School in 1947. An accomplished athlete, James was co-captain of the Williston High School basketball team (1945) and captain of the Williston baseball team (1946–47).

During his childhood, he met Gladys Sutton, the daughter of Edward Sutton (a brakeman with the Atlantic Coastline Railroad) and Janie Thompson Sutton originally from Sampson County. After graduating from high school, Gladys attended Johnson C. Smith University in Charlotte, N.C., studying history and German. James, however, enrolled in the U.S. Air Force and, while assigned to the Hickam Air Base in Hawaii, again displayed his athletic skill – becoming the youngest airman to become captain of the Hickam Field baseball team.

After a brief career in the Air Force, James began his college training at North Carolina College (now North Carolina Central University). There he attended the John Hope Franklin Symposium. As he pursued studies in mathematics and chemistry, he spent his summers on the baseball diamond, as a member and later captain of the N.C. College baseball team, member of the Quebec and Ontario teams of the Canadian Baseball League, and as a member at varying times of the Wilmington Clippers, Durham Eagles and Kansas City Monarchs baseball teams. During this time, he married his childhood sweetheart, Gladys Sutton, who was an educator in the Onslow County School system at the time. Although that marriage later ended in divorce, two children were born to them – a daughter, Cynthia Brown, B.S., M.S. (Phillip) and a son, Michael, B.S., chemical engineering (Tarita).

James Brown initially pursued a career in education, teaching high school science in Lilesville, N.C. and later mathematics at Williston Junior High School. However, he quickly realized that career opportunities for him were very limited in Wilmington.

Following the path and inspiration of African-American medical trailblazers in Wilmington such as Dr. Leroy Upperman and Dr. Frank Avant, he accepted a post as the first African-American Senior Mathematician at the Naval Ordinance Laboratory in White Oak, MD in 1957. This led to an appointment in 1959 as a research assistant under Dr. Edward Hawthorne, Chairman of the Physiology Department at Howard University in Washington, D.C.

This all motivated James to pursue the doctor of medicine degree and in 1963, it was bestowed upon him by Howard University. Upon achieving his M.D. he became licensed to practice in the states of Maryland and North Carolina as well as the District of Columbia. Following an appropriate internship and residency with St. Elizabeth's Hospital, he was appointed their Senior Medical Officer.

It was during this time that he met the lovely Vera Reese who had returned home to join the District of Columbia's Department of Public Health where she designed and implemented the department's first Disability Review Program. She earned her M.S.W. from Howard University and began her career as a clinical caseworker at Cleveland General Hospital. She continued at the Crile Veterans Administration Hospital and later served as Chief of the Community Support Program for the D.C. Department of Human Services. In 1968 she and James were married, to which union was born one daughter Kimberly Brown Smith, Ph.D., M.D. (Abel).

Brown maintained a private family medicine practice for almost 40 years while serving in other capacities including Assistant Clinical Professor of Family Practice, Howard University (1973–75); Proctor of the American Board of Family Practice, Howard University (1974); various posts as an officer of the Greater Southeast Community Hospital (1974–1992); Vice-chair of the Blue Cross & Blue Shield Credentialing Committee of the National Capital Area (1997–2003); and many other prestigious posts in and around the Washington, D.C. area. During his career, he has also published on numerous occasions and lectured on various medical topics.

Not forgetting the importance of giving back to one's community, he has maintained a lifetime membership in the NAACP, and has contributed to the support of his church, United Methodist Church of the Redeemer (Temple Hills, MD), the greater Southeast Community Hospital Auxiliary, N.C. Central University, the NMA (National Medical Association), Howard University Medical Alumni Association, the Williston Alumni Association and numerous other philanthropic causes. In 2006, United Methodist Church of the Redeemer recognized him with its Lifetime Achievement Award.

Realizing that a family is only as strong as each rung on its ladder, James Brown, M.D. has established another legacy for his family and community through his support of the 1898 Memorial Park. As his grandmother told him the stories of the great injustice which occurred in Wilmington in 1898, so he has continued the oral tradition and has begun a written chronicle by telling the story to his children and grandchildren. His goal is that we never forget, but that we use the knowledge to make our families stronger and to make our communities better. At the time of this printing, Dr. Brown continues to live in retirement with his wife Vera in Temple Hills, MD. He has visited Wilmington frequently over the years.

Founders Circle

David Jones
Wilmington Mayor 1999-2001

A native of New Bern, North Carolina, David Jones has established himself as a leader in business, government, and politics. He served as mayor of the City of Wilmington from 1999-2001 and is a former Secretary of the North Carolina Department of Corrections, where he served from 1972-1976.

As a businessman, Jones serves as president of David Jones Investments, Inc., owner of David Jones Rentals, LLC, and vice-president of Pawn USA, Inc.

He has served on numerous boards, including the UNCW Board of Visitors, the North Carolina Commission on National and Community Service, the UNCW Seahawk Club, Greater Wilmington Chamber of Commerce Committee of Local Government Affairs, the North Carolina Center for Public Policy Research, Training Board of the Salem Law Enforcement Academy, Elderhaus, and the YMCA of Fayetteville and Wilmington. One of the original founders of United National Bank, the only minority bank in eastern North Carolina, Jones has also served on the boards of directors of Branch Banking and Trust, Wilmington; Southern National Bank, and Peoples Trust and Bank.

His involvement in the community is far-reaching. In addition to endowments at the University of North Carolina Wilmington and Cape Fear Community College, he has supported Boys & Girls Homes of North Carolina, Boy Scouts of America, Brigade Boys and Girls Club, Children's Museum, Fellowship of Christian Athletes, Friends of Airlie Gardens, Cameron Art Museum, March of Dimes, New Hanover County Public Library, Rotary, Salvation Army, St. Jude's Children's Hospital, Southeastern Community College, Southeastern Sickle Cell, Special Olympics, United Cerebral Palsy, USS North Carolina Battleship, and the YMCA.

He is a recipient of the Razor Walker Award from the University of North Carolina Wilmington in recognition of distinguished service to the people of North Carolina.

He has two sons, Pete and Scott Jones, and four grandchildren.

Peace Circle

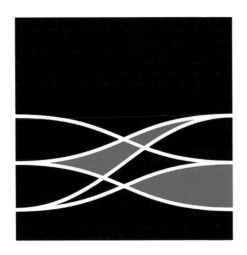

WACHOVIA

**Our mission is
to build strong and vibrant communities,
improve the quality of life,
and make a positive difference
where we work and live.**

The Wachovia Foundation is a private
foundation that is funded annually by
Wachovia Corporation.

Founders Circle

Celebrating an Enlightened Point of View

SunTrust is proud of the diversity initiatives we've implemented to raise the quality of our workforce and employee well-being. Recognizing and respecting the uniqueness of individuals is a way of life that directly affects the success of our business in an ever-expanding and competitive marketplace.

More than just race or gender, diversity can mean a single characteristic, experience, or idea that makes one person similar to or different from another.

At SunTrust, we are constantly striving to expand upon, learn from, and grow from these differences to ensure a responsive and supportive environment. We encourage several points of view to allow employees the freedom to maximize their contributions to our company, customers, and communities.

Sun Trust operates 1,678 retail branches and 2,509 ATMs in Alabama, Arkansas, Florida, Georgia, Maryland, Mississippi, North Carolina, South Carolina, Tennessee, Virginia, West Virginia, and the District of Columbia.

Founders Circle

History of
The Community Foundation of Southeastern North Carolina

The year was 1987. A gentleman named Dickson Baldridge moved to Wilmington from Fairfield, Connecticut to enjoy the Cape Fear area in his retirement. Once here he dove into community activities, for he was not the kind of man who enjoyed being idle.

He quickly realized that the Cape Fear region had neither a community foundation serving it, nor did anyone know about the powerful effects such a charitable organization could have on local philanthropy. He went to work seeking out community leaders and informing them about community foundations, since he was very familiar with them from his experiences back home.

Community foundations enhance the quality of life for all citizens within their service areas by using funds entrusted to its stewardship by people of all means. They are created to provide a permanent source of funding for charitable organizations. Publicly supported charitable entities themselves, community foundations function as a simple vehicle for thoughtful, broadly based, local philanthropy.

A feasibility study was conducted to determine if a community foundation should be started. The study showed that there was a strong consensus among community leaders, nonprofit agencies, and others that a community foundation for the Cape Fear area was both practical and doable.

Articles of incorporation and by-laws were signed on February 22, 1987, and filed with the North Carolina Secretary of State. The incorporators were Dickson Baldridge, Channing W. Daniel, Jr., Allene C. Keith, Esq., and Frank B. Gibson, Esq. The first board meeting took place on April 12, 1987, with 15 new directors in attendance. Five months later the organization received its official IRS designation as a tax-exempt nonprofit corporation. Originally known as the Wilmington Community Foundation, the name was quickly changed to the Cape Fear Community Foundation.

Early contributions totaled $2500 for operational expenses. Shortly thereafter the first perpetual endowment fund was established. The Community Foundation was on its way.

The Community Foundation's name was changed again in 2002 to the Community Foundation of Southeastern North Carolina in order to better reflect the five county area it served: Bladen, Brunswick, Columbus, New Hanover, and Pender.

THE
COMMUNITY
FOUNDATION
OF SOUTHEASTERN NORTH CAROLINA

Today the Community Foundation holds nearly $5,000,000 in assets, used to support the wide spectrum of charitable organizations throughout the Cape Fear region. In 2007 during the Community Foundation's 20th anniversary, it awarded more than $1,200,000 in charitable grants to hundreds of nonprofit agencies.

In 2001 the Community Foundation was privileged when it was asked to create the 1898 Memorial Fund with funds collected to erect a monument to commemorate the race riots of that year and to serve as a symbol reminding all of the importance of harmony today. The Community Foundation administered the 1898 Memorial Fund throughout the planning and construction of the Third Street park, for all to admire as they enter downtown Wilmington.

The Community Foundation is similar in some ways to the 1898 Memorial. It recognizes Wilmington's history while offering hope for its future.

Peace Circle

George Rountree III and Family

> If we are to achieve a richer culture,
>
> rich in contrasting values, we must
>
> recognize the whole gamut of hu-
>
> man potentialities, and so weave a
>
> less arbitrary social fabric, one in
>
> which each diverse human gift will
>
> find a fitting place.
>
> **Margaret Mead**

Peace Circle

Bank of America

Our Philosophy

"We believe,
very simply,
that it is the actions of individuals working together
that build strong communities ...
and that business has an obligation
to support those actions
in the communities it serves."

Kenneth D. Lewis, Chairman and CEO

At Bank of America, we are committed to creating meaningful change in the communities we serve through our philanthropic efforts, associate volunteerism, community development activities and investing, support of arts and culture programming and environmental initiatives.

Peace Circle

Hugh MacRae II and Family

HUGH MACRAE II is a native of Wilmington, North Carolina, and the son of Nelson MacRae and Marguerite Bellamy MacRae. Hugh spent his formative years in Wilmington and later graduated from St. Paul's School in Concord, New Hampshire. He then entered Princeton University for one year and left in 1943 to join the Army Air Corps in World War II, graduating from Flying Schools as a Second Lieutenant preparing for overseas duty in Europe, when the war ended in 1945. He returned to Princeton University in 1946, and after graduation from Princeton, he attended the University of North Carolina at Chapel Hill receiving a degree in Business Administration. At Princeton, Hugh earned his varsity letters for athletics in ice hockey and crew.

After graduation from college, Mr. MacRae entered business in Wilmington with his grandfather, the senior Hugh MacRae, in the real estate development business, building residential and commercial properties in Wilmington, Wrightsville Beach, and Linville Resorts in western North Carolina. Following the death of the senior MacRae in 1951, Hugh MacRae II organized The Oleander Company, Inc., to continue the family business in the same real estate developments. These projects included, among others, Hanover Center, Independence Mall, Oleander, Lincoln Forest, and Wrightsville Beach.

In addition to his business activities, Mr. MacRae has found time to hold the following civic activities and positions:

President, Trustees, James Walker Memorial Hospital

Vestry Member, St. James Episcopal Church

Chairman, Bellamy Mansion, Inc. (Historic Preservation)

Chairman, Military Affairs, City of Wilmington

Vice President, North Carolina Board of Realtors

Director, Wachovia Bank & Trust Company, Wilmington

President, Clan MacRae Society of North America

Honorary Chairman, American Red Cross Campaign

President, Wilmington Board of Realtors

Foundation University of North Carolina

Defense Orientation Conference Association Washington

Area Representative, Princeton, St. Paul's School

Mr. MacRae's outside interests and activities have been skiing, physical fitness, shooting, travel, photography, flying, family activities and golf. Within his golf activities, he has won amateur championships and he enjoys a membership in the Royal and Ancient Golf Club of St. Andrews, Scotland.

During the last thirty years, Mr. MacRae is proud of his military support and liaison work with the U.S. Marines at Camp Lejeune and U. S. and Royal Navy ship visits at Wilmington, North Carolina. He has received the following honors and citations:

Meritorious Service Citation received from the U. S. Chief of Naval Operations

Commendation from Commander-in-Chief Royal Navy aboard Carrier HMS Ark Royal in New York

A second commendation from Commander-in-Chief Royal Navy

Superior Service Citation from the U. S. Navy Department and the Commandant of the U.S. Marine Corps

Razor Walker Award

The Paul Harris Fellowship Award from the Rotary Club for community relations

Mr. MacRae also considers his most valuable assets to be his family and the activities of which the following accounts will describe.

EUNICE TAYLOR MACRAE – Mr. MacRae is married to Eunice of London, Ohio. Throughout her years in Wilmington as Mrs. MacRae, Eunice has served as Chairman of the Board of Trustees of the University of North Carolina at Wilmington and has held numerous board positions including the Children's Museum, the Bellamy Mansion, and the Advisory Board of the Duke Medical Center Cancer Clinic Advisory Board and others. Mrs. MacRae enjoys many activities with her friends including golf and bridge, at which she is an expert player.

Within the MacRae family, the following children have taken their place with great love, pride, and affection as follows:

RACHEL CAMERON MACRAE, born in Wilmington, NC, attended public schools until she entered and graduated from Garrison Forest School in Baltimore, Maryland. Rachel then attended Hollins College and graduated from Salem College. After residing in Charleston, South Carolina for a number of years, where she received a Master's Degree in Psychology at Citadel College, she has returned to Wilmington. For several years, Rachel has served as a Psychological Counselor at the University of North Carolina at Wilmington and, more recently, she has entered private practice on her own. A charming and spirited girl, her many interests include horseback riding, golf, and activities with family and friends. Rachel has also traveled extensively in America and Europe, and she often visits with her aunt and uncle who live in England near London.

HUGH MACRAE III, the elder son, attended public schools in Wilmington, and Cape Fear Academy, Episcopal High School in Washington, and graduated from the University of North Carolina at Chapel Hill. After several years of working in real estate with the Intracoastal Corporation, Hugh has joined the family company, The Oleander Company, and works with his father and his brother in the various real estate development and management activities. Hugh is married to his lovely wife Ann and they have two children, Daniel Nelson MacRae and Ann Christine MacRae, who are beautiful additions to the MacRae family. Father Hugh greatly enjoys his family activities, water sports, and maintaining a lovely home and grounds on Greenville Sound. Within his civic activities, Hugh has served as president of the YMCA of Wilmington.

NELSON MACRAE - After attending public schools and Cape Fear Academy, Nelson graduated from the University of North Carolina at Wilmington. Thereafter, Nelson entered the family business, The Oleander Company, where he has participated fully in the management of the Company and is now serving as president.

Within his outside activities, Nelson serves as a member of the board of Wachovia Bank in Wilmington and a board member of Coastal Land Trust. He has been a leader in placing family properties and others on the west bank of the Cape Fear River and on Town Creek under conservation easements, which will hold these properties in a natural state, without development, which is of tremendous public benefit.

Nelson's personal interests include golf, shooting, family activities and the management of the beautiful family property, Old Town Plantation on the Cape Fear River, which is under conservation protection. He also continues these activities in western North Carolina at Linville, where he manages family properties there.

Nelson is married to his lovely wife, Elizabeth, and they have a handsome son, Nelson MacRae III. A second child is almost here, and our prayers are that this will happen safely and happily.

MARGUERITE BELLAMY MACRAE, the youngest MacRae, born in Wilmington, was educated in local schools and graduated from St. Paul's School, Concord, New Hampshire. She then graduated from Sarah Lawrence College in New York. Meg MacRae is a charming, intelligent, adventurous girl who has worked in Wilmington in the movies for the *Dawson Creek* series. After this, she moved to Los Angeles, California, to expand her activities in the movies and popular music.

Her latest employment has been production manager of the world famous Eagles Band, with whom she has traveled and managed in many European and American cities. Her employment with the Eagles now keeps Meg busy full time and her main recreation is to visit at home in Wilmington where her prime enjoyment is relaxing at the family cottage on Wrightsville Beach, where she enjoys beach and water activities. Meg also has substantial concern for persons who are underprivileged and handicapped. She believes that the Lord has put her on this earth to find ways to help less fortunate people.

Founders Circle

A Pioneer for Civil Rights

Lisbon Berry Jr.

1922-1995

Whether in private practice or as a senior trial attorney with the U.S. Department of Justice or as executive director of Legal Services of the Lower Cape Fear, Lisbon Berry championed civil rights for the poor and downtrodden. He successfully argued the case of Aaron McRae before the New Hanover County Board of Education, which kept two separate school systems. This 1962 case caused the board to reverse its decision and admit McRae to Chestnut Street School - the first black to enter an all white school in the history of New Hanover County. During the 1960s when Berry served as the East Coast cooperating attorney for the NAACP Legal Defense and Educational Fund, Inc., his leadership prevented police brutality of more than 200 demonstrators who had been arrested and charged with criminal trespassing.

Prior to opening a law office in Wilmington, North Carolina, Berry was a partner with the late Floyd McKissick Sr. in the firm of McKissick & Berry in Durham, NC. At the time of Berry's move to Wilmington, there was only one other black lawyer in town (Robert Bond). In 1967, Berry accepted an appointment as trial attorney with the U.S. Department of Justice, which increased to five the number of black lawyers in the Civil Rights Division. Throughout Alabama, Georgia, Florida, Illinois, Indiana, Louisiana, and Mississippi, Berry was a member of teams that investigated, tried, and convicted violators of civil rights acts. He tried school desegregation, voting rights, and employment discrimination cases. His work in public accommodations cases earned him commendations from the attorneys general of several administrations.

In 1982, Berry retired from the Department of Justice and returned to Wilmington where he became Executive Director of Legal Services of the Lower Cape Fear. In 1987, he retired a second time from legal practice, devoting many hours to the local community. He served on several boards and commissions, including the study commission for the consolidation of Wilmington and New Hanover County governments. He also worked for the establishment of the New Hanover Airport Commission and was a member and chair of the Community Boys and Girls Club, and a member of the board of Community Penalties. He was a life member of the NAACP. In addition to his advocacy for civil rights for all, he had a passion for the arts and was seen often at local theatrical productions and was a board member of the Thalian Hall

Center for the Performing Arts as well as member and president of Friends of Public Radio (WHQR). Berry served as an elder at Chestnut Street Presbyterian Church where he also sang in the Men's Choir. Additionally, his church work included Vice-Moderator of the Nomination Committee of Coastal Carolina Presbytery.

Lisbon Berry Jr. was born April 1, 1922, in Washington, DC, the first child of Lisbon C. and Annie Evans Berry. His sister, Josephine Berry Johnson, during World War II, served as Director of the Negro USO in several southern cities, including Wilmington. She was selected to open the USO office in Lawton, Oklahoma, where she still resides. His late brother, Charles Evans Berry, was a renowned tenor who toured Germany and Western Europe, for more than 10 years, performing as Sportin' Life in *Porgy and Bess*.

Lisbon Berry was a graduate of Williston Industrial School, North Carolina College for Negroes (now North Carolina Central University) and Howard University School of Law. His children are Shepsara Amenam Howard (nee Deborah Berry), Lisbon C. Berry III; and Kimberly Berry, Esq. His widow, Shirley Hart Berry, a New Jersey native, continues to live in Wilmington where she is active with the Guardian ad Litem Program, as an advocate for abused and neglected teenagers who are in the legal system through no fault of their own. Having earned a graduate degree from Georgetown University (Washington, DC), she taught in the District of Columbia public schools and several North Carolina colleges, retiring after ten years from the English Department at Cape Fear Community College.

Peace Circle

New Hanover County Community Action

For more than 40 years, New Hanover County Community Action, Inc. has served the Wilmington community by educating and uplifting economically disenfranchised citizens in an effort to make permanent improvements in their health and lifestyles.

It was during the 1960s that grassroots activists such as John H. McCoy, Samuel Hicks and many others saw new opportunities to gain support in their work to help economically disadvantaged citizens improve their plight. President Lyndon Johnson's "war on poverty" offered new federal funding direct to communities for programs like Workforce Investment, JTPA Job Training, Community Service Block Grants, and Head Start.

In 1967 a small group of community activists successfully petitioned the federal government for funds to launch a Head Start project in Wilmington. Head Start was designed to give low-income children ages 3-5 years old a "head start" in gaining the academic skills necessary to succeed in school. However, Head Start did not begin and end with the child. Embracing the program's core philosophy, the entire family was embraced to ensure that parents could grow in sync with their child's growth. The program's design offered comprehensive health, nutrition, dental, mental health and social service support to families of enrolled children.

The first year of the project proved unsuccessful. Refusing to accept failure, John H. McCoy garnered support from local politicians and businessman including Attorney Bruce Jackson to reapply for federal funding of the project. A second opportunity was granted in the following year to the fledgling group, and a formal board of directors was established. Initial funding was for approximately $10,000.

Several churches and community organizations rallied in support of this new program. A lack of facilities made capital a major priority in the early days. The Hillcrest community, St. Stephen African Methodist Episcopal Church, St. Mark's Episcopal Church and the New Hanover County Board of Education were among a few in the community to answer the call for partnership and aid. By 1986 the Head Start program's funding level had grown to just under $200,000, but was still very meager when measured against the total resources need to successfully administer the program.

The 1980s brought further challenges and opportunities. As demand for the program increased, it was inevitable that the board of directors could not continue to operate without a headquarters facility and satellites in the county. In 1986, with support from then state Senator Frank Block, Attorney Bruce Jackson and U.S. Congressman Charlie Rose, the board of directors obtained the former Peabody Elementary School building. With federal and private aid, the building was refurbished to meet state, local and federal minimum requirements for operation as an early childhood development center. The Rock Hill Community Organization and Turnkey community under the leadership of Emerson Whitted and George McClammy also responded to the call providing the agency with partnerships to reach needy families outside the inner city core.

It was also during this era that through the vision of John H. McCoy, the board of directors obtained new funding to enhance its approach to combating poverty in the community. New programs were established and by 1991, the agency re-incorporated to become New Hanover County Community Action, Inc. New programs were created in addition to Head Start, including the CSBG Adult Self-Sufficiency Project, Home Weatherization, Heating and Air Conditioning Repair and Replacement, GED (in partnership with Cape Fear Community College), FUTURE (father involvement program), Wrap Around Before and After School Services for young children and Survival Skills Training for Men, Women, and Teens. In addition the agency partners with the local Smart Start Office and New Hanover County Schools as a More-At-Four state-funded preschool site, as well as many other community organizations striving to serve disadvantaged citizens and their children.

In 2007 the agency was named the New Hanover County Human Relation Commission's "Organization of the Year." Executive Director Cynthia Brown hypothesized that many of the agency's clients are likely 1898 descendants considering a by-product of the wrath of social, political, and economic disengagement can be families not realizing their genealogy. To this end, it has made the work of New Hanover County Community Action, Inc. in this new century more important than ever.

Upon the death of founding board member John H. McCoy in November, 2007, the agency renewed its spirit and commitment to educating and uplifting the disenfranchised members of the community. Through the support of the cornerstone churches of Campbell Square where the agency's headquarters facility is located – First Baptist, St. Stephen AME, Chestnut Street Presbyterian, and St. Mark's Episcopal – New Hanover County Community Action, Inc. continues its legacy of providing support to ensure the well being of Wilmington's African-American community.

The 2008 Executive Officers and staff include Clarence Smith, Board Chairman; Rev. Charles Davis, Vice-Chairman; James Moore, Treasurer; Candace Artis, Secretary; Kenneth Davis, Parliamentarian; and Cynthia Brown, CEO and Executive Director.

Clarence L. Smith - Board Chairman
2006 - 2008

Cynthia J. Brown - Exec. Director / CEO
1998 - Present

Peace Circle

Local 1426, 1935-2008

The History of the International Longshoremen's Association

Local 1426 was begun as a result of a unique friendship between a dentist, a funeral director, and an I.L.A. vice president. While attending an Elks convention in 1935 at Wilson, NC, a Dr. Avant encountered George Millener, an ILA vice president at Hampton Roads, Virginia, and told him the plight of the un-unionized Wilmington longshoremen.

Joseph Ryan , the ILA International president, upon hearing of the Wilmington longshoremen's desire to become organized, dispatched ILA vice president Jerry Jones of Gulfport, Mississippi, accompanied by a Mr. Fox, a professional organizer of the AFL-CIO, to Wilmington.

At their initial meeting, Dr. Avant and the late Ted Sadgwar's Funeral Home advanced the money to assist them in securing a charter. At the Loving Union Hall, these first officers were elected: John Phillips, president; John Miller, financial secretary; Hamie Thomas, treasurer; John Sheridan, recording secretary. This particularly promising leadership was interrupted by death, with Ben Hooper replacing John Phillips as president and Herman Sykes serving as the vice president. The following year Sykes replaced Mr. Hooper as president.

Since its establishment in 1935, the ILA Local 1426 has operated out of several locations in Wilmington, including Love & Charity Hall in the 600 block of Harnett St., Ruth Hall at 7th & Nun, Old Community Hospital at 7th & Red Cross, and in the Old Building at 314 Harnett St.

The present building at 1305 South Fifth St. was dedicated on April 30, 1967. The building was soon named the Rutherford B. Leonard Labor Temple in honor of Billy Leonard who made enormous contributions toward the growth and development of Local 1426.

The Labor Temple has been an institution in Wilmington's African-American community, hosting numerous social gatherings, weddings, banquets, funerals, and church services.

The Labor Temple is the headquarters for organized labor in southeastern North Carolina.

Present officers include John Bellamy, Jr., president; Gregory Washington, vice president, Lewis Hines, Jr., business agent; Michael L. Dinkins, secretary-treasurer; Kenneth Grady, recording secretary; Harrison Richardson, marshall; and the Rev. Johnny Wise, chaplain.

Peace Circle

Wilmington Chapter of The Links, Inc.

In the fall of 1946, two women in Philadelphia, PA invited seven of their friends to discuss a new type of club for African-American women in the aftermath of World War II. Those women, Margaret Roselle Hawkins and Sarah Strickland Scott, envisioned a need for a different organization from the existing Greek letter sororities that would provide leadership in postwar America, and address concerns of civil rights and racial injustices. Through their friendship, they envisioned a three-fold service objective to promote civic, educational and cultural concerns. That meeting launched what is now known as The Links, Incorporated, an international women's organization of more than 10,000 women of color. The organization is based on friendship and driven by the desire to be of service to the community.

In Wilmington, NC, women with similar vision and stance were ignited by the same sparks of friendship to heed the call to service in a new way. As word spread friend to friend of the newly established organization, Wilmington, NC became the 15th chapter in the country to be chartered and recognized as a member of The Links, Incorporated's chain of friendship.

Under the visionary leadership of Celeste Burnett Eaton* (wife of Dr. Hubert Eaton) the Wilmington, NC Chapter was chartered in 1951. The other women who joined with her were Evelyn Carnes*, Leonard Green*, Louise Moore*, Iris Jeffries Wade North*, B. Constance Odell, Catherine Robinson*, Elizabeth Green Holmes Saulter*, Mabel Spaulding*, and Jean Williams*. Although many were spouses of influential men in the community, they were accomplished women in their own rights within the business, educational, medical and other disciplines. To that end, they worked energetically to realize the goals of the national organization through service in the local community.

The work of these women left an indelible mark on the effects of the 1898 Massacre in Wilmington for they worked tirelessly to educate the masses and to uplift the talent in the African-American community. New standards of civic responsibility for the community were established through the work of the Wilmington chapter of The Links, causing a change in the course of local history.

Following the national platform for service delivery, the Wilmington chapter has focused its energy in four areas: the Arts, International Trends and Services, National Trends and Services and Services to Youth. Individual members as well as the collective membership have contributed to the community financially, in service and through collaborative partnerships with others. Just a few examples of the organization's impact on the local community include: sponsorship of the annual Kaleidoscope Fine Arts Brunch which showcases local African-American talent in the visual and performing arts; development of the video "Talented Tenth: Heritage Rediscovered' to promote a deeper understanding of local African-American history; mentoring and awarding of scholarships to academically gifted African-American students in need of financial support; philanthropic efforts including Gala 2000, from which proceeds were donated in support of the Zimmer Cancer Center at New Hanover Regional Medical Center; and partnerships with the Wilmington Symphony to expose and enrich the community's awareness of the rich African-American influence on classical music.

In 2007, the Wilmington chapter was nominated for and received the New Hanover County Human Relation Commission's Organization of the Year Award. However, the Links' work in the 21st century has included building new bridges between our community and other cultures. Educational and medical support for children and families in Belize, Haiti, West and South Africa, and Panama has increased through the efforts of the local chapter and its members.

The Wilmington chapter continues its legacy of doing good each year for those in need. Chapter officers in 2008 include Cynthia Brown, president; Laura Lynn Allen, vice-president, Glancy Thomas, treasurer, Mercedes Newsome, financial secretary, Annie Hill, recording secretary, Gloria Monroe, corresponding secretary, Attorney Charlene Richardson, parliamentarian, and Wanda J. Sloan, protocol officer.

Peace Circle

LS3P/
BONEY ARCHITECTS

LS3P/**BONEY**
2528 Independence Blvd.
Suite 200
Wilmington, NC 28412
Ph 910.790.9901
www.LS3P.com

Founders Circle

Leslie N. Boney, Sr. (1880-1964) moved to Wilmington from Wallace in rural Duplin County at the end of World War I, and worked on the design and construction of Hanover High School for Florence architect W.J. Wilkins. Following completion of that project, Boney joined local architect Henry Gause as an apprentice, and established his own firm following Gause's death in 1922. His early work in Wilmington included schools, churches, houses, and the grey stone addition to the New Hanover County Courthouse. Working with Wilmington's Public Housing Authority, he designed Jervay and Taylor Homes in the late 1930's and 1940's in an effort to improve the quality of housing for the City's underprivileged.

Boney's five children grew up in Wilmington through the Depression and attended public schools. His oldest daughter, Mary Boney Sheats, became a Bible scholar and author for the Presbyterian Church, and retired as Director of Bible Studies from Agnes Scott College in Decatur, Georgia. Leslie Sr.'s three sons (Leslie N. Boney, Jr., William J. Boney, Sr., and Charles H. Boney, Sr.) became architects and returned to work for their father after World War II. Sue Boney Ives, his youngest daughter, worked for the firm as secretary and office manager.

Leslie N. Boney, Sr. and his children valued education and sought opportunities to improve it - through their architecture - across North Carolina. They were missionary in their zeal for this work, traveling the length of the State by car, bus, or train, and much later by plane, in an effort to provide architectural services for a growing North Carolina Public School system. The firm's work during the first half of the twentieth century provided schools for many rural communities in the era of "separate but equal" education systems. Many of these early schools remain in use today as testimony to their ability to work for - and importantly with - both African American and white educators who valued education for all.

Three members of the third generation of the Boney family (Paul Davis Boney, Charles H. Boney, Jr., and Christopher Lawrence Boney), with the same belief in the value of education, now move forward as LS3P/BONEY, joined by many other partners across North and South Carolina. We are proud to help fund this important 1898 Memorial Park to commemorate a challenging period in our nation's history.

In this Memorial we acknowledge the past, celebrate the advancements of education and opportunity in the intervening years, and look forward to a future we now build together as a single community, brick by brick, person-to-person, hand in hand.

LS3P/BONEY

Paul Davis Boney, FAIA   Charles H. Boney, Jr., AIA   Christopher L. Boney, AIA

SOME OF OUR MOST
IMPORTANT CONNECTIONS
TO THE COMMUNITY
AREN'T FOUND ON
UTILITY POLES.

At Progress Energy, we're as connected to the people of our communities as we are to the homes and businesses we serve. That's why we constantly work to support and sustain our area through outreach projects, educational grants, environmental stewardship and economic development. In short, electricity is just the beginning of the energy we bring to the community.

LOOKING AT POWER IN A NEW LIGHT.

Founders Circle

BB&T is honored to support the 1898 Memorial Park Foundation.

"BB&T's dedication to the community is evident by the involvement of its many employees in various community activities sponsored by BB&T. These activities relate to economic development, health care and human services, youth and education."

Wilmington Area Executive Phil Marion

BB&T opened its first office in Wilmington, NC, in 1984, and constructed a new main office in the coastal city in 1987.

Today, BB&T operates 12 branches in Wilmington and northern Brunswick County, with plans to open its 13th branch in the fall of 2008.

Founders Circle

BRANCH·BANKING·COMPANY

A Sound Heritage
Upon opening its doors in 1872 in
the town of Wilson, North Carolina,
the predecessor of BB&T Corporation
began its evolution from a private
institution serving the surrounding
agricultural area to today's multibillion
dollar financial services company
ranking 14th in asset size among
the nation's banks. BB&T has always
been more than brick and mortar;
our very foundation is built on values
and vision.

The healing continues

STATEWIDE DISCUSSION: *Star-News* Publisher Robert J. Gruber appeared on a UNC-TV panel with then N.C. Rep. Thomas Wright and Orage Quarles III, publisher of the *Raleigh News & Observer*, to discuss what the media should be doing to comply with recommendations from the 1898 Commission.

SPECIAL PUBLICATION: The *Star-News*, in partnership with the *Charlotte Observer,* the *News & Observer* and Dr. Timothy Tyson, published a special section, "1898 Remembered," in November 2007 to describe what happened 110 years earlier and to bring about a greater understanding of our shared past.

LEADERSHIP DEVELOPMENT: In 2004 and 2005, the *Star-News* sponsored a leadership development program called Focus on Leadership for minority members of the community. Graduates from these two classes have gone on to assume leadership positions on boards, commissions and committees throughout Wilmington and the surrounding area.

BUSINESS DEVELOPMENT: For two years, *Star-News* Publisher Robert J. Gruber served as a board member of Partnership for Economic Inclusion, a group of black and white businesspeople founded in 1998 to help bring economic parity to minority-owned businesses in the Wilmington area. In early 2008, that group folded its efforts into other thriving organizations, such as the Black Chamber Council of the Greater Wilmington Chamber of Commerce and the regional Inclusion Coalition Board.

NEWS COVERAGE: In January 2005, the *Star-News* hired a reporter to cover African-American issues as part of her beat. Angela Mack took on the challenge enthusiastically and methodically, introducing herself to leaders in the community, arranging meetings with organizations such as the NAACP and Commission on African-American

A s the oldest continuously published daily newspaper in North Carolina, the *Star-News* holds a distinctive place in the history of our community. The newspaper was founded in 1867 by William H. Bernard, a Confederate veteran, and during the 1898 riots, headlines reflected the views of white Democrats.

Today, 140 years later, the *Star-News* strives to be a voice for an increasingly diverse population and to help heal the wounds from a turbulent past – injustices that demand acknowledgement and reconciliation.

Toward these ends, the *Star-News* has taken several concrete steps to build a better relationship with the African-American community.

with lessons learned.

History. Her work has helped the *Star-News* provide information both for and about the black community. It also has balanced the paper's coverage with a sustained focus on positive inclusion.

Highlights of the *Star-News'* coverage:

■ Ongoing coverage of the 1898 Wilmington Race Riot Report, detailing the deadly violence inflicted by white mobs on successful black residents and their white allies.

■ Stories commemorating the 35th anniversary of the Wilmington 10 – black and white students

wrongly imprisoned for racial unrest that occurred during desegregation of the city's public schools in 1971. Dr. Benjamin Chavis-Muhammad, who led the protests and was one of the people falsely imprisoned, sought out Angela for an exclusive interview.

■ A front page dedicated entirely to black community leaders on Martin Luther King Jr. Day in 2007.

■ An examination of how and why Wilmington's

black population declined in the past five years.

■ A series during Black History Month in 2007 profiling important figures in history.

JOURNALISM WORKSHOPS: In 2007, the *Star-News* held two journalism workshops that involved minority youth.

■ **Photographer Briana Brough** created a three-week photography program for children who reside in the Creekwood Housing Development.

Briana mentored students in the classroom and took several groups out on location to photo shoots. The students captured images that were printed as a photo spread in the

newspaper and as an audio slideshow online. The program was very positive for the students and they produced several impressive images.

■ **Reporters Angela Mack and Tyra M. Vaughn** led a second workshop focused on giving minority youth hands-on experience in news writing and one-on-one interaction with reporters. Seven students from New Hanover and Hoggard high schools attended the workshop for two hours after school for a week at the newspaper offices at 1003 S. 17th St. The workshop inspired some to join their school's newspaper staff and take a closer look at journalism as a future career.

Founders Circle

For more 'Star-News' coverage of 1898 and the work of the 1898 Commission, visit www.StarNewsOnline.com/1898. Though reprints of the 1898 special section are no longer available, you may download a copy at www.StarNewsOnline.com/1898.

The History of R. S. Jervay Printers, The Cape Fear Journal and the Wilmington Journal

"We integrated the public library with one phone call and the city golf course by the simply going out to play there one day."

Thomas C. Jervay

The patriarch of North Carolina's Jervay family of journalists lived an American success story life. No newspaper man himself, the Rev. William R. Jervay (1847–1910) set a standard for leadership and learning for his children when such things were denied African-Americans in the South during the late nineteenth century and early 20th century. Jervay was born a slave on the Gabriel Manigault rice plantation in South Carolina from which he fled to fight for the Union Army in the Civil War.

After the war, he returned to South Carolina, where he purchased and operated a large farm in St. Stephen Parish. He represented Berkeley County in the constitutional convention of 1868, and served in the South Carolina House of Representatives from 1868 to 1872, and the Senate from 1872 to 1876. He was also auditor for the city of Charleston and a lieutenant colonel in the

state militia. In 1874, he was elected vice-president of the South Carolina Republican Convention. He learned the skills of a carpenter and prized education for his children. He sent his son, Robert Smith Jervay (1873–1941), to Charleston's Avery Institute and then to Claflin University in Orangeburg, S.C.

William spent the remainder of his years as an African Methodist Episcopal minister in Beaufort and Summerville, S.C. His commitment to religion became a family trait. Indeed, churches were at the core of many African-American communities in the segregated South, and those who rose to leadership positions often did so through church connections. Not surprisingly, one of the first printing assignments that helped launch the Jervay family into journalism was the publication of a church newspaper, the *Christian Star*.

It was William's son, Robert, who printed the church paper and founded the R. S. Jervay Printing Company and the *Cape Fear Journal*. Robert was born in Summerville, and following his education, he moved in 1892 to the Elbow Community in Columbus County. He worked as the bookkeeper and manager of the commissary for a lumber company, and it was from there that he printed church programs and newspapers. In 1894, he married schoolteacher Mary Alice McNeill of Wilmington in her parents' home at 417 South 7th Street across the street from where The *Wilmington Journal* is presently located.

In 1898, Robert S. Jervay was named Elbow's postmaster. Three years later in 1901, he established the R.S. Jervay Printing Company. Like his father, Robert wanted his children (ten in all) to receive a good education, and in 1911, he moved his family and his printing business to Wilmington. The children attended the Gregory Normal Institute. Their mother, Mary Alice graduated from Gregory in 1892.

The printing business was a family enterprise and mostly manual. The press was hand-fed and the type was set by hand. Mary Alice served as a typesetter and proofreader. Her sons—Henry, Paul, and Thomas—worked in various capacities. Thomas Clarence "T. C." Jervay recalled his job as an eight-year-old, delivering on his bicycle the printed minutes of fraternal and civic organizations.

The 1920s were a tumultuous time for race relations in the South, and there were few outlets for African-American opinion. Henry encouraged his father to begin a newspaper for blacks in the Wilmington area. Wilmington had not had a black newspaper since the destruction of Alex Manly's *Daily Record* in the *coup d'etat* of 1898. In 1898, Mary Alice's parents and siblings lived next door to the Manly press and one of her siblings was banished from Wilmington. In February of 1927, the family began publication of the *Cape Fear Journal*, a four-page weekly tabloid that sold for a nickel. "T. C." Jervay sold the first paper. A year later, the Jervays purchased a linotype machine and a flatbed press to print the paper. The dominant, white-owned newspaper, the *Wilmington Star*, praised the weekly in a 1929 editorial as "one of the most constructive Negro papers in the South."

The Depression brought hard times for everyone, and the Journal struggled like other businesses. It suspended publication in 1930 for several months but was back on the streets by October of that year.

Thomas C. Jervay was a 1932 graduate of Williston Industrial High School, where he edited the *Williston Echo*. He was the first recipient of the North Carolina Mutual Life Scholarship. The class of 1932 was the first class to graduate in eleven years due to the Great Depression. He went on to attend Hampton Institute and Howard University and received a Bachelor of Science degree from Virginia State University. He served on the newspaper staff at all three universities and returned to Wilmington in 1937 to work as business manager and editor of the *Cape Fear Journal*. His brother Paul moved to Raleigh and founded the *Carolinian*.

When Robert died in 1941, T.C. assumed the leadership in the business, renaming the newspaper the *Wilmington Journal* in 1945. He became publisher and editor upon the death of his mother, Mary Alice, in 1948. Like his parents, "T.C." and his wife Willie made the newspaper a family enterprise that would be handed down to their children.

The *Wilmington Journal* became influential in North Carolina during the second half of the century because of its outspoken positions during the civil rights movement and their unique expansion into other towns and cities. "T.C." became a champion for civil rights for African-Americans in Wilmington. In an August 1953 edition of the *Journal*, long before antidiscrimination laws and "affirmative action" hiring policies, "T.C." called on the city of Wilmington to employ black firemen and policemen, and asked voters to elect blacks to the city council, board of education, and the city's housing authority. He also spoke out for more affordable housing for blacks, paved streets in black neighborhoods, and a black-owned drug store and supermarket. In the years leading up to the civil rights movement of the 1960s, the newspapers also dealt with the events of everyday life of African-Americans in Wilmington and southeastern North Carolina. Along with the local headlines were success stories and achievements of blacks on the state, national, and international scene.

"T. C." personally led the effort to integrate the public library and the city golf course. He was a local leader in the NAACP and motivated black business people to pay the costs for the first African-American (retired Judge Ernest Fullwood) to enter Wilmington College in 1962. The state's new Human Relations Commission selected "T.C." in 1963 to receive a Community Service Award. He was president of the National [African-American] Newspaper Publishers Association.

The influence of the *Journal*, however, can be determined in part by the fear it provoked in its enemies. One such enemy was a white supremacist named Lawrence Little, who, in 1973, used nine sticks of dynamite to blow up and set fire to the *Journal's* building. Jervay and his family had once lived above the paper's office but had moved. Little was caught and convicted, and Jervay attributed the bombing to his newspaper's tradition of defending the rights of black people especially those of Ben Chavis and Kojo Nantambu, co-ministers, at that time, of the Temple of the Black Messiah. "They blasted my shop, but we never missed an issue," he said later.

"T. C." Jervay spent a lifetime in journalism and was enshrined in 1999 into the National Newspaper Publishers Association Black Press Archives at Howard University. The same year, he was inducted posthumously into the North Carolina Journalism Hall of Fame at the University of North Carolina at Chapel Hill. He was eulogized as "a media man in the best tradition" during the funeral service on Friday, December 31, 1993. He died Tuesday December 28, 1993, at the age of 79. A tribute to his life, written by former *Wilmington Journal* staff writer Rhonda Bellamy and submitted by U.S. Representative Charlie Rose, Congressman, was entered into *The Congressional Record*, Washington, D.C., February 1, 1994, Volume 140, Number 6.

The newspaper passed on to his heirs. Ms. Willie Jervay, T.C.'s widow, is now the publisher emeritus. His daughter, Katherine, is retired after 29 years of service in the business, where she served as co-publisher and business manager. Daughter, Mary Alice Jervay Thatch is presently editor and publisher. Grandchildren Shawn Thatch, Robin Allen, and Johanna Thatch Briggs work in various capacities. And great-grandson Jonathan Allen works in layout.

Presently, The *Wilmington Journal* continues to be the voice of the African-American community. His heirs have held on to the direction voiced by "T.C." Jervay and are carrying on the legacy.

The Daniels Family

A native of Winter Park, Florida, **Windell Daniels** (1947-2008) graduated from Jones High School in 1965. He joined the U.S. Marine Corps and served most of his time in Vietnam and in the Mediterranean Sea as a combat engineer. After fulfilling his duties as a staff sergeant, he joined the Marine Corps Reserve and remained active for nine years. He earned an associate's degree in General Occupation Social Technology from Cape Fear Community College in 1980. Windell retired in 1985 from Koch Fuel, where he was plant manager for 14 years.

He began his entrepreneurship in real estate by purchasing houses and renovating them. He later purchased the 1904 William Hooper School and converted it into a 22-unit apartment complex for the elderly and a 23-unit complex for moderate to low income residents, now known as the William Hooper Apartment Complex. Windell was also president of United National Tours, LLC and Daniels Development Company, LLC, and founder of United National Masons and Order of Eastern Stars.

Windell served as president of the Greater Wilmington Chamber of Commerce and the Community Boys and Girls Club, chairman of the Wilmington Housing Authority Board of Commissioners and acting executive director, founding board member of Cape Fear Bank, and a member of the UNCW Board of Trustees, North Carolina Funeral Board Service, Wilmington Sportsman Club, the USS SSN777 Committee, Greater Wilmington Sports Hall of Fame, and the North Carolina Economic Development Commission. He also served as co-chairman of the City of Wilmington's 10-Year Plan to End Homelessness and chairman of Housing Economic Opportunities, Inc. In recognition of his civic service, he received the *Star News* Lifetime Achievement Award and the Daniels Production Company Lifetime Achievement Award.

The son of Elease Johnson Daniels and the late Rufus Daniels, Windell is survived by his wife of 38 years, Wilma Daniels, and two sons, Windell and Euran Daniels, both of Raleigh.

Wilma Daniels, a 1969 graduate of Hoggard High School, earned a B.S. in Business Management from Shaw University in 1992. She retired from Hoechst Celanese as purchasing agent after 26 years and is presently vice president of Daniels Development Company, LLC, co-founder of William Hooper Apartments, LLC, and vice president of United National Tours, LLC. Wilma serves on the UNCW Board of Trustees and the boards of New Hanover Community Health Center, Greater Wilmington Chamber of Commerce, and Cape Fear Community College Foundation. She serves as vice chair of the Wilmington Black Chamber of Commerce. A past board member of the YWCA of the Lower Cape Fear, Wilma is founder of the Katherine Smith Finley Endowment and is a graduate of Leadership Wilmington. Honors include induction into The Order of Cape at Cape Fear

Community College and a 2008 Lady of Legacy Award. She is the daughter of the late Katherine Smith Finley and Eddie Williams.

Wilmington native **Windell Jamar Daniels** graduated from Laney High School in 1989. He is a 1995 graduate of Fayetteville State University, where he earned a bachelor's degree in computer science. He has worked as a project manager for IBM for 13 years, and has received an Outstanding Achievement Award, Commitment to Quality Award, Bravo Award, and Customer Satisfaction Award. He is president of Symon'e Tours, LLC. He is married to Cheryl Denise Daniels (11 years). The couple's children are Tania Symon'e Daniels and Christopher Jamar Daniels.

A 1994 graduate of Laney High School, **Euran S'car Daniels** holds a B.A. from North Carolina State University. He is president of Daniels Production Company, LLC, Daniels Tours, LLC, and Daniels Creative Consulting, LLC. He has worked as a project manager for IBM for 13 years and was executive producer of the television program Teens –N- Progress. Euran became the youngest person in the history of UNCW to establish an endowment, the Euran S. Daniels Scholarship Endowment. He has received numerous commendations, including North Carolina Triangle Black Achievers Award, Black Entertainment Television's Teen Summit Youth of the Month Award, and *YSB Magazine's* Top Ten Teens of America Award.

The late **James Daniel Finley** was president of the first commercial driving school in the state of North Carolina. In addition to Finley's Driving School (located on Davis Street in Wilmington), he also owned Chartered Coach Service, Finley's Gas Station, and Finley's Auto Sales. A native of Kingston, GA, he was married to the late Katherine Smith Finley for 35 years. Their children include Leon Williams, Wilma Williams Daniels, and Jesse Smith.

Peace Circle

Founders Circle

BB&T

LS3P/BONEY ARCHITECTS

DR. JAMES BROWN

HUGH MACRAE II

PROGRESS ENERGY

IN MEMORY OF ALICE MOORE SISSON

SUN TRUST BANK

WACHOVIA FOUNDATION

SARAH LEE WHITE

WILMINGTON *STAR NEWS*

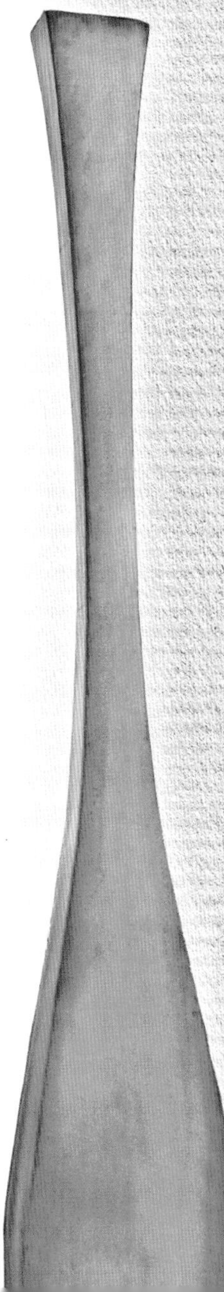

Peace Circle

BANK OF AMERICA

IN MEMORY OF
WILLIAM (BILL) D. BRYANT
BY THELMA, TANYA, TAWANA
AND JOE

COMMUNITY FOUNDATION OF
SOUTHEASTERN NC

IN MEMORY OF
WINDELL DANIELS
BY WILMA W., WINDELL J., AND
EURAN S.

HISTORIC WILMINGTON FOUNDATION

IN MEMORY OF
S. J. HOWIE, JR.
BY LYDIA, SAMUEL, III, AND HERSCHEL

ILA LOCAL 1426 WILMINGTON, NC

DAVID L. JONES

IN MEMORY OF
SEN. LUTHER H. JORDAN, JR.
BY KISHA

THE LINKS, INC., WILMINGTON, NC
CHAPTER

MINISTERIAL ROUNDTABLE

NEW HANOVER COUNTY COMMUNITY
ACTION, INC.

PPD

SYLVIA AND GEORGE ROUNTREE, III

LINDA UPPERMAN SMITH

BARBARA SULLIVAN AND MICHAEL
MURCHISON

IN MEMORY OF
ERNEST A. AND JEFFRIE SWAIN

BERTHA BOYKIN TODD AND FAMILY

CHARLIE WEST AND BEVERLY CREE

Hope Circle

AFRICAN-AMERICAN HERITAGE FOUNDATION

SEYMOUR AND MILDRED ALPER

ALPHA PSI OMEGA-AKA, INC.

VALERIE AND DON BETZ

ANN AND JULIA BOSEMAN

SPENCE & KIMBERLY BROADHURST

IN MEMORY OF
DEUMPHFORD AND THELMA BULL
(BY LIZZIE, COLLIN, SONJA AND ALAN)

BETTY H. CAMERON

DAVID CECELSKI AND TIMOTHY TYSON

CHESTNUT STREET PRESBYTERIAN CHURCH-
USA

IN MEMORY OF WILLIAM D. CHILDS

COOPERATIVE BANK

CORNING INCORPORATED

FRANCINE DECOURSEY

DELTA SIGMA THETA SORORITY

ANGELA W. AND JAMES H. FAISON, III

FIRST BAPTIST MISSIONARY CHURCH

KATHLEEN AND MICHAEL GLANCY

PETER GREAR, ESQ.

LETHIA SHERMAN HANKINS

LINDA AND HAMILTON HICKS, JR.

IN MEMORY OF
MARY MARLENE JACKSON (MOTHER)
MARGIE MCALLISTER-JACKSON (SPOUSE)
LAWRENCE LOCKHART (FRIEND)

INDEPENDENCE MALL

IN MEMORY OF
REV. J. ALLEN KIRK, D.D.
(CENTRAL MISSIONARY BAPTIST CHURCH)

LANDFALL FOUNDATION

JAMES LEUTZE AND MARGARET GATES

MACEDONIA MISSIONARY BAPTIST CHURCH

GERRY MCCANTS

CONGRESSMAN MIKE MCINTYRE

MELTON AND SANDRA MCLAURIN

JAMES AND MARJORIE MEGIVERN

LEE AND GLORIA MONROE

WALLACE C. MURCHISON

NEW BRIDGE BANK

LAURA W. PADGETT

PARTNERS FOR ECONOMIC INCLUSION

DAVID AND CARY PAYNTER

RESIDENTS OF OLD WILMINGTON, INC.

THE ROCK OF WILMINGTON

ANNE RUSSELL

ST. MARY CATHOLIC CHURCH

ST. STEPHEN AME CHURCH

BILL & RENEE SAFFO

ROBERT R. AND MYRTLE B. SAMPSON

THOMAS AND CATHERINE SCHMID

EARL AND SANDRA SHERIDAN

SHILOH MISSIONARY BAPTIST CHURCH

SHERMA SVITZER

WALKER TAYLOR AGENCY, INC

UNIVERSITY OF NORTH CAROLINA
WILMINGTON

HANNAH VAUGHAN AND NORMAN ROBINSON

IN MEMORY OF DR. WILLIAM JAMES WHEELER

A. WILLIAMS TAX EXPRESS, INC

WILMINGTON CHAMBER OF COMMERCE

MARY AND CLAUDE YOUNG, SR.

Unity Circle

DR. & MRS. LEON ANDREWS

DONN ANSELL

FOUNTAIN FINANCE ASSOCIATION

ADKINS-DRAIN FUNERAL HOME

MS. SONYA J. BENNETONE

MRS. KATHERINE L. BICK

JUDGE REBECCA W. BLACKMORE

MR. & MRS. FRANKLIN L. BLOCK

MRS. LILLIAN B. BONEY

MS. BERNADETTE H. BOYCE

DERRICK EDISON BOYKIN

R. C. BOYLAN

MR. & MRS. SID BRADSHER

IN MEMORY OF JOHN H. BREWINGTON
(BY LOUISE BREWINGTON)

JOHN M. BROOKS

A. BROWN

PHILLIP & CYNTHIA B. BROWN

MR. AND MRS. PHILLIP J. BROWN

MS. BILLIE A. BURNETT

GILBERT H. BURNETT

MS CAROLINE K. BUTTS

WILLIAM 'BILL' CASTER

DR. AND MRS. S. CLAYTON CALLAWAY, JR.

MRS. CAROLYN K. CAMPBELL

STERLING & KIMBERLY CHEATHAM

MS. GENEVA P. CLARK

DRS. PHILLIP & CASSANDRA CLAY

COASTAL CHIROPRACTIC CENTER
DR. PHILIP VANCAMPEN

CAPTAIN CLARENCE C. & DIANE U. COOPER

COOPERATIVE BANK

COPY CAT PRINT SHOP

CORBETT INDUSTRIES, INC.

MR. & MRS. RUSSELL CORBETT

J. P. CREDILE

K. W. DANIEL, JR.

G. S. DIAB

MRS. ALLENE DRAIN

MRS. HILDA CAMERON DILL

MRS. L. B. DEAN & M. A. FREEZE

IN MEMORY OF SALLYE DUDLEY
(BY WILLIAM H. DUDLEY SR., SHAUNTA, WILLIAM JR.,
SHAINA & WILLIAM III)

MR. & MRS. THOMAS J. EAGER

EBENEZER MISSIONARY BAPTIST CHURCH

MR. & MRS. CLDYE C. EDGERTON

MS. CAROLE W. ELLIS

ELIZABETH'S PIZZA

MR. & MRS. MACK FORD

FOUNTAIN FINANCIAL ASSOCIATES

MR. & MRS. MICHAEL A. FREEZE II

JUDGE ERNEST FULLWOOD

F. E. FUNK

DR. ROGER GAUSE

REV. A.L. GEE

GIBSON'S ACCUPRINT

DR. BETTIE J. GLENN

JUDGE PHYLLIS GORHAM

MARY & DEAN GORNTO

DR. DAN & KAREN GOTTOVI

PROFESSOR WILLIAM B. GOULD IV

MRS. CONSTANCE DRAIN-GREENE

MS. KATHERINE M. GRIFFIN

REV. PERRY D. & RITA TODD-GRIFFIN

MS. LAURIE GUNST

OTIS & ELIZA JEAN HAMES

HANOVER REALTY, INC.

HAROLD'S HOME & HARDWARE

MR. & MRS. B. WILSON HARDY

GEORGE HAWES

JOHN H. HAYLEY III

CAMILLA HERLEVICH & JAMES T. BRIER

MS. M. F. HEYWARD

MS. MAE HIGH

HORACE MANN INSURANCE COMPANY (JOHN
BROOKS)

KSG HOUSE

MR. & MRS. EUGENE HUGELET

JACSON W. BEVERAGE

MS. GERALDINE JOHNSON

MS. JOYCE JOHNSON

MR. & MRS. RON E. JOHNSON

MS. MABLE JUSTICE

DR. WILLIAM KASSENS

IN MEMORY OF EDDIE J. KEITH
(BY JEANNE KEITH HARRIS)
(DR. DARRYL KEITH & FAMILY)

KEN WEEDEN & ASSOCIATES, INC.

RUSSELL J. LABELLE

MS. BOBBIE J. LINEBERGER

REV. WAYNE LOFTON & FAMILY

BECKY LONG AND HARRY MARRINER

LONGORDO'S APPLE ANNIE'S

JAMES R. MACRAE

MS. LINDA J. MACRAE

ANDRE & MARY MALLETTE

MS. GUSSIE WYLENE MAPSON

R. W. MARRIOTT

DR. MAURICE MARTINEZ

MRS. LORENA B. MCBROOM

DR. STEPHEN MCCARY-HENDERSON

MS. MILDRED MCDONALD

R. S. M. MCGLADREY

HARRIS & LAURA MCINTYRE

DR. & MRS. ERIC MCKEITHAN

MR. & MRS. HERBERT P. MCKIM, JR.

MS. CHRISTINE B. MCNAMEE

MICKEL'S HAIR DESIGN (C. DAWSON)

H. MILLER

MR. & MRS. F. WAYNE MORRIS

FERNE L. MOSLEY, ATTORNEY

MS. ROSALIND M. MOSLEY

J. S. MURCHISON

MS. MARGUERITE MURRAIN

MS. IVY MURRAIN

DR. SAMUEL & JOYCE MURRELL

R. NATHANSON

C. R. NEAL

MS. DOROTHY B. NESBITT

MR. & MRS. LAVAUGHN NESMITH

MRS. MERCEDES J. NEWSOME

N. C. MUTUAL LIFE INSURANCE COMPANY (FOUNDED 1898)

MS. DEIDRE MCKELLAR O' BRYANT

REV. & MRS. ARTIE ODOM, JR.

K. ONO

MS. BETTY PARKER

MS. MARGARET H. PARRISH

MS. LINDA PEARCE

HARPER PETERSON

D. M. & H. M. PICKARD

S. M. PICKARD

C. PIERCE

MR. & MRS. H. D. POLLACK

S. QUINN

RAE'S BEAUTY HUTT (W. RAE HILL)

ATTORNEYS TERRY & CHARLENE RICHARDSON

MR. & MRS. R. S. RIPPY

MR. & MRS. CHARLES RIESZ

MR. & MRS. C. RIESZ, JR.

MR. & MRS. JAMES E. RICE

MR. & MRS. JAMES H. ROBINSON

K. ROBINSON

DR. KENNETH & PATRICIA ROBINSON

ROD'S AUTOMOTIVE, INC.

MR. EARL & NATALIE HINTON-STALLING

R. I. SALWITZ

D. SCARAFONI

JANET K. SEAPKER

MR. & MRS. DAVID G. SEIPLE

D. A. SHERMAN

REV. HENRY SMITH

MS. VIRGINIA P. SNEED

ST LUKE AMEZ CHURCH

STATE FARM INSURANCE (HANK BROWN)

BEN STEELMAN

CHARLES & DR. RACHEL STEPHENS

R. C. STEPHENS

THE STERLING HOUSE

TETTERTON & OPHEIM

THETA KAPPA OMEGA

ROBERT & GLANCY THOMAS

RUDY P. THURMAN

TREMAN & TREMAN, D.D.S.

CAPTAIN BRIAN EDWARD TODD (DELTA AIRLINES)

KATHLEEN C. BERKELEY & HARRY TUCHMAYER

UNCW OFFICE OF CAMPUS DIVERSITY

VIDEO LINE PRODUCTIONS

JOHN D. WALSH

MS. GERTRUDE MOORE WADDELL

JOHN WASSON

MR. & MRS. HENRY WEYERHAEUSER

WILMINGTON SPORTSMAN'S CLUB

MS. EVA T. WILLIAMS

OTIS L. WOOD

Friends Circle

ACME ART, INC.
MR. & MRS. MICHAEL C. ADAMS
DR. AUDREY C. ALBRECHT
J. A. ALFORD
M. AKIL
MR. & MRS. R. BAIN
MS. LOLITA BENNETT-BRYANT
BETH & GREG BELL
JANE D. BECKHAM
BETA SIGMA PHI SORORITY
MS. AVA P. BEVINS
K. L. BICK
MILTON BLUE
L. N. BONEY, JR.
BETTY BOWDEN
MR. & MRS. ALLAN BOYD
H. J. BRACKETT
JAMES & LYDIA BRAYE
J. G. BRISTER
MS. CHARLENE BROWN
D. D. BROWN
MR. & MRS. JEFFREY S. BRUNER
JEANNE "SALLY" CASE
KRISTEN T. CAVANAUGH
JUDGE & MRS. W. ALLEN COBB, JR.
EDNA NEAL COLLINS
W. H. CONSER
BILL COPELAND
MR. & MRS. RUSSELL CORBETT
DAVID R. CORLEY
MICHAEL & LINDA CREED
MS. VIVIAN CROSBY
LEROY & HARRIETT CRUMMY
M. W. CUNNINGHAM
C. B. DAVIS
JIMMY DAVIS
NATASHA N. DAVIS
NICOLE L. DAVIS
CLYDE & BARBARA DINKINS
RICHARD D. DIXON
C. B. DODSON
DOTTIE'S BEAUTY COURT
CHRISTOPHER F. DUMAS
MS. ADDIE N. DUNLAP
MS. LETHETTA FORBES
MITCHELL RAY FOWLER
M. O. FRYAR
MR. & MRS. PHILIP FURIA
CARL & DEBBIE GALBREATH
DR. ROGER GAUSE
FRANK B. & JUDITH R. GIBSON
DR. JOHN L. GODWIN
MS. PHYLLIS H. GUBERMAN
SOLOMAN J. GUBERMAN
AGATHA H. HAGEPANOS
G. HAWKINS
MR. & MRS. DEXTER HAYES
MR. & MRS. SHERMAN HAYES
MR. & MRS. R. W. HAYWOOD
M. M. HIGHFILL
MS. ALICE HOLMES
M. J. HOWIE
IN MEMORY OF R. H. HOWIE
R. R. HOWIE

C. HOYLE
PAUL JEFFERSON
D. C. JONES
DR. & MRS. BERT P. JOHNSON
J. KAPRA
MR. & MRS. JOHNATHON KELLEY
F. LAMB (MAYO)
JAMES D. LEONARD
PATRICIA L. LEONARD
DR. & MRS. JACK B. LEVEY
LOCK AND KEY SHOP
SALLY JOY MACKAIN, PH.D.
ELIZABETH MARTIN
MS. DEBORAH MAXWELL
MR. & MRS. WM. F. MAYO
M. L. MCEACHERN
DR. & MRS. S. MCGARRITY
BARBARA MCKENZIE-TERVO
TERESA MCLAMB
J. A. L. MILLER
MR. & MRS. GILL MINOR
CATHERINE F. MORRIS, CPS
B. J. MOSCOSE
MR. & MRS. R. TERRY MOUNT
J. R. MURCHISON
LINDA & REID MURCHISON
DR. & MRS. N. MURRELL
J. W. MYERS
MS. CAROLYN NELSON
J. FRED NEUBER, JR
MS. KATIE C. NIXON
MS. MARY NIXON
MARY ANN K. NUNNALLY
MR. & MRS. ARTHUR W. O'CONNOR
S. M. PICKARD
MR. & MRS. JAMES PIERCE, JR.
S. A. PROCTOR
W. A. RANEY
MS INEZ RICHARDSON
P. M. RIGG
HELEN & DOROTHY ROMEO
D. G. SEIPLE
MR. & MRS. RONALD K. SIZEMORE
STEPHEN A. & TRACY E. SKRABLE
WILLIAM & GAIL SLOANE
B. LYNN SMITHDEAL
MS. VIRGINIA P. SNEED
RICHARD & TRISH SNYDER
J. M. SWART
M. R. THOMPSON
P. (ACME) TOLL
E. T. TOWNSEND
PAMELA S. TRUNKEY
T. H. VADEN
MS. FRANCIS VAUGHN
RICHARD WARREN
DR. & MRS. JACK WILHEIM
MR. & MRS. PAUL WILKES
DONALD WILLIAMS
KATHERINE J. WINTERS
MS. MARY WILSON
P. H. WOOD
J. L. WORZEL

Community Supporters

Pam Adams

Annie Artis

Glenn Barefoot

Wilma Bell

John Bennett

Wendy Block

Carl Brown

Cynthia Brown

Ren Brown (late)
Memorial Selection Panel

Ayers Burgess

Billie Burnett

Gilbert Burnett

Liz Buxton

Carl Byrd

The Rev. Johnny Calhoun
Ministerial Roundtable Co-chair

Anne Canada

Si Cantwell

Caronell Chestnut

Richard & Patricia Cliette

The Rev. Joseph Cooper
Ministerial Roundtable

Mimi Cunningham

Harry Davis
1898 Artist

Trish Doyle

Pamela O'Brien Eldridge

Carol Ellis

Diane Emerson

Corey Evans

Don Fishero

Grenoldo Frazier

Margaret Fredlaw

Margaret Freeman (late)
Director of "No More Sorrow to Arise"

William Freeman

Bessie Funderburg (late)

Philip Gerard

John Godwin

Father Thomas Hadden

Ken Hatcher

Margaret Herring

Brenda Hicks

Elizabeth Hines

The Rev. Marcellus Howard

David Hume

The Rev. Lone Jensen
Ministerial Roundtable

Bill Jessup

Dionne Johnson

Frankye Manly Jones
Honorary Co-chair
1898 Memorial Park Campaign

Sen. Luther Jordan (late)
Honorary Co-chair
1898 Memorial Park Campaign

Susan King

Rowan LeCompte

Ken Lemon

Dr. James Leutze

Tony Lofton

Diane Lomax

Hugh MacRae
Honorary Co-chair
1898 Memorial Park Campaign

Connie Majure

Connie Mantis

Gerry McCants

Sandra McClain

The Rev. William McDow

Herb McDuffie (late)

The Rev. Ron McGee

Joyce Mims

Katherine Moore

Meg Mulrooney
Historian

Wallace Murchison
Study Circles Co-Chair

Catherine Myerow

Jean Nance

Orlando Newkirk

Jonathan Noffke

Maxwell Paige

Yvonne Pagan

Linda Pearce

Lorraine Perry

Larry Price

Allen Randall

Marc Recko

Terry Richardson

Tony Rivenbark

Dave Robertson

Samuel Rose

George Rountree

Faith Davis Ruffins
Memorial Selection Panel

Anne Russell
Memorial Selection Panel Chair
Playwright - "No More Sorrow to Arise"

Peggy Schroeder

The Rev. William Seibert

Jean Shapiro

Imam Abdul Shareef

Virginia Sherman

Georgia Smallman

Anita Smith

Bertha Smith

Dentral Smith

W.A. Soders

Sandra Spaulding-Hughes
Memorial Selection Panel

Virginia Stewart

Katherine Taylor
Honorary Co-chair
1898 Memorial Park Campaign

Beverly Tetterton

Rita Todd

Willie Vereen

B. Constance Waddell
Study Circles Co-Chair

Sharon Wade

James Wall

The Rev. Anthony Watson

Rabbi Robert Waxman
Ministerial Roundtable

Dale Wright
1898 Reenactor

Thomas Wright

Peter Zukoski

Bibliography

Suggested Reading

Anderson, Eric. *Race and Politics in North Carolina, 1872-1901: The Black Second*. Baton Rouge: Louisiana State University Press, 1981.

Bellamy, John D. *Memoirs of an Octogenarian*. Charlotte: Observer Printing House, 1942.

Byrd, John Timothy. "The Disfranchisement of Blacks in New Hanover County, North Carolina." Microfilm LD3941.8 R63 1998 Reel 1, University of North Carolina at Wilmington.

Cecelski, David S. and Timothy B. Tyson, eds. *Democracy Betrayed: The Wilmington Race Riot and Its Legacy*. Chapel Hill: University of North Carolina Press, 1998.

Cody, Sue Ann. "After the Storm: Racial Violence in Wilmington, North Carolina and Its Consequences for African-Americans." Master's thesis, University of North Carolina at Wilmington, 2000.

Connor, R.D.W. *The Life and Speeches of Charles Brantley Aycock*. Garden City, N. Y., Doubleday, Page & Co., 1912.

Crow, Jeffrey J. "Cracking the Solid South: Populism and the Fusionist Interlude." In *The North Carolina Experience*, eds. Lindsey Butler and Alan Watson. Chapel Hill: UNC Press, 1984.

Crow, Jeffrey J. and Robert F. Durden. *Maverick Republican in the Old North State: A Political Biography of Daniel L. Russell*. Baton Rouge: Louisiana State University Press, 1977.

Dancy, John Campbell. *Sand Against the Wind: The Memoirs of John C. Dancy*. Detroit: Wayne State University Press, 1966.

Daniels, Josephus. *Editor in Politics*. Chapel Hill: University of North Carolina Press, 1941. See chapter 26: "The White Supremacy Campaign."

DeRosset, William L. *Pictorial and Historical New Hanover County and Wilmington, North Carolina, 1723-1938*. Wilmington, N.C., 1938.

Edmonds, Helen G. *The Negro and Fusion Politics in North Carolina, 1894-1901*. Chapel Hill: University of North Carolina Press, 1951.

Evans, William McKee. *Ballots and Fence Rails: Reconstruction on the Lower Cape Fear*. Athens: University of Georgia Press, 1995.

Gilmore, Glenda E. *Gender and Jim Crow: Women and the Politics of White Supremacy in North Carolina, 1896-1920*. Chapel Hill: University of North Carolina Press, 1996.

Glancy, Michael L. "The Wilmington Riot of November 10, 1898." Research report, University of North Carolina at Wilmington Multiple Abilities Program, 1973.

Godwin, John L. *Black Wilmington and the North Carolina Way: Portrait of a Community in the Era of Civil Rights Protest*. Lanham, Maryland: University Press of America, 2000.

Greenwood, Janette T. *Bittersweet Legacy: the Black and White "Better Classes" in Charlotte, 1850-1910*. Chapel Hill: University of North Carolina Press, 1994.

Hamilton, Joseph G. de Roulhac. *Reconstruction in North Carolina*. New York: Columbia University Press, 1914.

Hayden, Harry. *Story of the Wilmington Rebellion*. Wilmington, N.C.: Harry Hayden, 1936.

Hayden, Harry. "History of the Wilmington Light Infantry." Unpublished Manuscript held at the New Hanover Public Library.

Higuchi, Hayumi. "White Supremacy on the Cape Fear: The Wilmington Affair of 1898." Master's thesis, University of North Carolina at Chapel Hill, 1980.

Hodges, Alexander Weld. "Josephus Daniels, Precipitator of the Wilmington Race Riot of 1898." Honors essay, Department of History, University of North Carolina at Chapel Hill, 1990.

Hossfeld, Leslie H. *Narrative, political unconscious and racial violence in Wilmington, North Carolina.* New York: Rutledge, 2005.

Hossfeld, Leslie H. "They Say the River Ran Red with Blood: Narrative, Political Unconscious and Racial Violence in Wilmington". General Collection F264.W7 H68 2003a. University of North Carolina at Wilmington.

Justesen, Benjamin R. *Black Tip, White Iceberg: Black Postmasters and the Rise of White Supremacy in North Carolina, 1897-1901. North Carolina Historical Review* 82 no. 2 (April 2005), pp. 193-227.

Kenzer, Robert C. *Enterprising Southerners: Black Economic Success in North Carolina, 1865 - 1915.* Charlottesville: University Press of Virginia, 1997.

Kirk, J. Allen. *Statement of the Facts Concerning the Bloody Riot in Wilmington, N.C., of Interest to Every Citizen in the United States.* Wilmington, N.C. J. Allen Kirk, 1898. http://docsouth.unc.edu/nc/kirk/menu.html

Kirshenbaum, Andrea M. "Race, Gender, and Riot: The Wilmington Race Riot of 1898." Honors essay, Duke University, 1996.

Kirshenbaum, Andrea Meryl. "'The Vampire That Hovers Over North Carolina': Gender, White Supremacy, and the Wilmington Race Riot of 1898." *Southern Cultures* 4, no. 3 (1998): 6-30.

Kornegay, Ralph B. *The Wilmington Riot, November 10, 1898.* General Collection F263.5 .K6, SENC-Books F263.5 .K6, University of North Carolina at Wilmington.

Kousser, J. Morgan. *The Shaping of Southern Politics: Suffrage Restrictions and the Establishment of the One-Party South, 1880-1910.* New Haven: Yale University Press, 1974.

Kraft, Andrew C. "Wilmington's Political-Racial Revoluton of 1898: A Geographical and Cartographic Analysis of the Wilmington North Carolina Race Riot." Honors Paper, University of North Carolina at Wilmington, 1993.

Lefler, Hugh T., ed., *North Carolina History Told by Contemporaries.* Chapel Hill: UNC Press, 1934. See pp. 397-400.

McDuffie, Jerome, A. "Politics in Wilmington and New Hanover County, North Carolina, 1865-1900: The Genesis of a Race Riot." 2 vols. Ph.D. dissertation, Kent State University, 1979.

McDuffie, Jerome A. "The Wilmington Riots of November 10, 1898". University of North Carolina at Wilmington.

McLaurin, Melton. "Commemorating Wilmington's Racial Violence of 1898: From Individual to Collective Memory." *Southern Cultures* 6, no. 4 (2000): 35-57.

Nash, June. "The Cost of Violence." *Journal of Black Studies* 4 (1973): 153-184.

Perman, Michael. *Struggle for Mastery: Disfranchisement in the South, 1888-1908*. Chapel Hill: UNC Press, 2001. See chapter 8: "Defeating Fusion II: North Carolina, 1898-1900."

Powell, William, ed., *Dictionary of North Carolina Biography*. 6 vols. Chapel Hill: University of North Carolina Press, 1979-1996.

Powell, William S. *North Carolina through Four Centuries*. Chapel Hill: University of North Carolina Press, 1989.

Prather, H. Leon, Sr. *We Have Taken a City: Wilmington Racial Massacre and Coup of 1898*. Cranbury, N.J.: Associated University Press, Inc., 1984. Reprint. Wilmington, N.C.: Nu World Enterprises, 1998.

"Race Riot of 1898." *North Carolina Literary Review* 2 (Spring 1994): 69-118.

Reaves, William M. *"Strength Through Struggle: The Chronological and Historical Record of the African-American Community in Wilmington, 1865-1950*. Edited by Beverly Tetterton. Wilmington, N.C.: New Hanover County Library, 1998.

Rippy, J. Fred, ed. *F.M. Simmons: Statesman of the New South*. Durham: Duke University Press, 1936.

Rivers, Patrick. "Unholy Minglings: Miscegenation and the White Revolution in Wilmington, North Carolina, 1898-1900". Microfilm LD3941.8.R63 1998 Reel 1. University of North Carolina at Wilmington.

Shapiro, Herbert. *White Violence and Black Response, from Reconstruction to Montgomery*. Amherst: University of Massachusetts Press, 1988.

Smith McKoy, Sheila. "Riot : Episodes of Racialized Violence in Africa and African-American Culture". General Collection PS374.N4 M38 1994, Microfilm PS374.N4 M38 1994. University of North Carolina at Wilmington.

Smith McKoy, Sheila. "When whites riot : writing race and violence in American and South African cultures". General Collection E184 .A1 S664 2001, SENC-Books E184 .A1 S664 2001, University of North Carolina at Wilmington.

Sprunt, James. *Chronicles of the Cape Fear River, 1660-1916*. Raleigh: Edwards & Broughton Printing Co., 1916.

Steelman, Joseph Flake. "The Progressive Era in North Carolina, 1884-1917." Ph.D. Dissertation, University of North Carolina, 1955.

Thomas, Larry Reni. "A Study of Racial Violence in Wilmington, North Carolina Prior to February 1, 1971." Master's Thesis, University of North Carolina at Chapel Hill, 1980.

Tyson, Timothy B. *Blood done sign my name : a true story*. Crown Publishing Group, 2005.

Umfleet, LeRae. *1898 Wilmington Race Riot Report*. Wilmington Race Riot Commission and the North Carolina Office of Cultural Resources, 2005. http://www.ah.dcr.state.nc.us/1898-wrrc/report/report.htm

Waddell, Alfred M. "Some Memories of My Life". General Collection E664.W115 A3, SENC-Books E664.W115 A3. University of North Carolina at Wilmington.

Watson, Jr., Richard L. "Furnifold Simmons and the Politics of White Supremacy." In *Race, Class and Politics in Southern History: Essays in Honor of Robert F. Durden*, Jeffrey Crow et al., eds. Baton Rouge: LSU Press, 1989.

Williamson, Joel. *The Crucible of Race: Black-White Relations in the American South Since Emancipation.* New York: Oxford University Press, 1984.

Wooley, Robert, H. "Race and Politics: The Evolution of the White Supremacy Campaign of 1898 in North Carolina." Ph. D. Dissertation, University of North Carolina at Chapel Hill, 1977.

Novels

Bland, Celia. *The Conspiracy of the Secret Nine.* Silver Moon Press, 1995.

Chesnutt, Charles W. *The Marrow of Tradition.* Houghton, Mifflin, 1901

Gerard, Philip. *Cape Fear Rising.* John F. Blair, 1997.

Thorne, Jack [pseudeonym for David Bryant Fulton]. *Hanover, or, The Persecution of the Lowly, a Story of the Wilmington Massacre.* Ayer Publishing, 1969.

Other Resources

1898 Centennial Foundation Commemoration Documents Special-Manuscript MS 217. University of North Carolina at Wilmington. Contains the official records of the 1898 Centennial Foundation, newspaper clippings about the commemoration activities, and some photocopies of reference materials about race relations and the 1898 racial violence.

The 1898 Wilmington Racial Violence and Its Legacy [video recording] : A Symposium. F263.5 .E53 1998 (5 video cassettes). University of North Carolina at Wilmington A video presentation of 1998 UNCW symposium lectures on the 1898 *coup* in Wilmington, North Carolina.

Confronting Dangerous Memories : Wilmington's Centennial Commemoration of the Coup of 1898. SENC-Books F264 .W7 C66 1999. University of North Carolina at Wilmington.

DeCoursey, Francine. *Remembering 1898: Moving Forward Together, Wilmington, North Carolina: A Community Effort Toward Reconciliation.* A/V Videocassettes F263.5 .R45 2002, SENC-Video F263.5 .R45 2002. University of North Carolina at Wilmington.

Russell, Anne. No More Sorrow to Arise. SENC-Books F263.3 .N67 1998, University of North Carolina at Wilmington. 1898 commemorative drama staged at Thalian Hall, 1998.

1898 Commissioned Artist - Harry Davis

Index

About the Editor
Rhonda Bellamy

Rhonda is news director for Cumulus Broadcasting, where she is heard daily on WGNI (102.7 FM), WMNX (97.3 FM), and "On the Waveline with Rhonda Bellamy," a daily talk show on politics and current events on WAAV (980 AM). She has formerly served as a staff writer for the *Wilmington Journal* and executive director of the Black Pages Publishers Association. She has garnered numerous commendations for her work from the Associated Press, including Best Newscast and Best Consumer Reporting. She is also the recipient of the Woman of Achievement Award in Arts from the YWCA, Woman of the Year by the New Hanover County Human Relations Commission, Community Hero by the New Hanover Community Health Center, and Citizen of the Year from the Wilmington chapter of the Winston-Salem State University Alumni Association. Rhonda also served as the official Mistress of Ceremonies for the 59th Annual North Carolina Azalea Festival.

A founding board member of the Black Arts Alliance, Inc., Rhonda serves as president and chairs the organization's signature Cine Noir Festival of Black Film. She has served on the Mayor's Task Force on Arts and Cultural Affairs under Mayor Harper Peterson, and is a past board member of Cameron Art Museum and the Wilmington Children's Museum. She is a founding teacher at the Dream Center for Arts Education where she presently teaches Readers' Theater and creative writing.

Rhonda presently serves on the board of directors of Cape Fear Habitat for Humanity after terms on the Domestic Violence Shelter and Services board, the City of Wilmington's African-American Heritage Commission, the Azalea Festival Multicultural Committee, and the Mayor's Convention Center Task Force under Mayor Hamilton Hicks.A native of New York, Rhonda graduated from Wilmington's E.A. Laney High School and is a graduate of North Carolina Central University, where she holds a B.A. in English with a concentration in Media/Journalism and graduate credits in Instructional Media.

She is the daughter of Ann and the late James McLaurin of Wilmington, mom to two young adults, and grandmother of one.

Assistant Editor

Si Cantwell is a local news columnist and Web site host for the *Wilmington Star-News*. His family has been in Wilmington for many generations, but he grew up in Charlotte and is a graduate of UNC-Charlotte. He started his career as night metro clerk at *The Charlotte Observer*, and worked in Miami, New Jersey and Pennsylvania before landing at the *Star-News* in 1990.

SlapDash Publishing, LLC

SlapDash Publishing is a publishing and design company located in beautiful Carolina Beach, North Carolina. Our focus is to preserve, promote and popularize our local history and culture in a graphically pleasing way that is both enduring and tastefully executed. We believe we have a unique capacity to present imagery and information in a tangible and effective way. Please visit our website for a list of distributors and to view some of our more recent work.

Daniel Ray Norris • www.carolinabeach.net • slapdashpublishing@me.com

Keep 9/2014

Keep 9/2014